THE COLLECTED
BEST OF WATERCOLOR

ROCKPORT

First published in the United States of America by
Rockport Publishers, Inc.
33 Commercial Street
Gloucester, Massachusetts 01930-5089
Telephone: (978) 282-9590
Fax: (978) 283-2742
www.rockpub.com

The work in this book originally appeared in *Best of Watercolor: Painting Texture*; *Best of Watercolor: Painting Color*; and *Best of Watercolor: Painting Light and Shadow*; selected by Betty Lou Schlemm and edited by Sara M. Doherty. Grateful acknowledgement is given to Betty Lou Schlemm and Sara M. Doherty for permission to reprint their work in this special edition.

ISBN 1-56496-876-6

10 9 8 7 6 5 4 3 2 1

Design: Kristen Webster–Blue Sky Limited
Cover Image: *Taos Autumn* by Gwen Fox

Printed in China

THE COLLECTED
BEST OF WATERCOLOR

GLOUCESTER MASSACHUSETTS

ROCKPORT

PUBLISHERS

Patio Patterns—Kathleen Pawley

SELECTED BY BETTY LOU SCHLEMM • EDITED BY SARA M. DOHERTY

INTRODUCTION

Rockport Publishers has been publishing The Best of Watercolor series for more than eight years. The original edition of *The Best of Watercolor* was published in 1993 and we received over 4,000 entries from watercolor artists all over the world. The judges, including Rockport's own Betty Lou Schlemm, spent weeks reviewing the submissions and agonizing over which 300 artists should be selected for the book.

Over the years, the judges have selected hundreds of talented artists for inclusion in the series. With each new edition, each artist's submissions become more inspiring than the last and the selection process becomes more difficult. *The Collected Best of Watercolor* is published in honor of the judges and watercolor artists whose hard work, talent, vision, and willingness to share their work have made The Best of Watercolor series a best-selling series for Rockport Publishers.

We dedicate this new edition to you—the hundreds of artists featured in The Best of Watercolor series over the years, and to all those artists who have yet to be featured.

Thank you,

Rockport Publishers

PAINTING COLOR

Color, of all design elements, has the greatest emotional impact. When we are dealing with color, as with music, we are dealing with sensations. It is not the objects that thrill us but that sensitive, imaginative way an artist puts them together and makes a personal statement in the world of art. Color plays upon form and defines it. It can move far back into the painting and then move forward, bringing into play the picture plane. The pictorial space is created with color; the reds advance, the blues recede, and the yellows sit right at our fingertips.

Harmonious colors, called analogous colors, fall close to each other on the color wheel, while contrasting colors, or complementary colors, fall opposite each other on the color wheel. Harmonious color combinations feel restful, while complementing colors add life to a painting and can feel lively or even shocking.

Value and intensity of color depend on the artist's feelings. Color changes as emotions change, and so do the many variations and combinations of value, hue, and intensity. Dull, murky colors, when combined with those of sheer brilliance, make bold colors sing, softly holding a painting together. Subtle gray washes will become rich if a few strokes of brilliant color are dropped into them when they are still wet. Together, a variety of colors work to make a beautiful piece of art.

Color composition is built with one stroke or shape against another until the entire painting is completely balanced. Color should stimulate the imagination. The warm colors, yellows, reds, and oranges, are exciting, but too much of these can leave a feeling of fatigue. But adding red, especially in moderation, can bring life and lift to a painting. Blues, greens, violets, and soft grays are emotionally restful. Merely venturing out under the blue, sunlit sky can be peaceful and restorative.

Color helps express all our emotions, and the knowledge of color and its power helps us in the pursuit of creating art. May this section's colorful paintings, of many styles and schools of thought, reveal each artist's quest in expressing personality in their creations with the use of color.

PENNY STEWART
Morning Glory
22" x 30" (56 cm x 76 cm)
Arches 300 lb. hot press

Using the language of color, I captured the beautiful serenity of this sunlit valley in the protective embrace of dark, silent woods. I first painted each foliage shape in its local color, and then added a second hue in the damp paint, enriching its color while suggesting both volume and texture. I was able to enhance the autumn beauty by contrasting light, transparent yellows and oranges with darker, more opaque greens and violets. To create variety and interest, I broke the larger field shapes into bands of green.

IRWIN GREENBERG
Street Musician
11" x 7" (28 cm x 18 cm)
Bristol 5-ply board

The model, a congo drummer, posed in my studio under a spotlight. His skin tone and outfit suggested the dominant warm color of the painting. The surrounding props were taken from sketches and painted to enhance the warm tones of the figure. The background was painted with cool tones, which contrasted with the warmth of the model and added vibrancy to the painting.

NANCY FELDKAMP
Harvest Ready
22" x 30" (56 cm x 76 cm)
Arches 140 lb. cold press

When planning a painting, I choose a triad of colors to use as a dominant theme and to ensure unity. With autumn's changing palette bringing greater color awareness, I used raw sienna, ultramarine blue, and alizarin crimson in *Harvest Ready* to suggest the season's sun-filled harvest weather. Other colors added accents and gave subtle variety to the shadows and negative areas of the painting. The paper remained unpainted in places to suggest the fields of near-white, ripened corn.

BRIAN DONN
Loquat Cascade
18" x 15" (46 cm x 38 cm)
Canson-Montval 140 lb. cold press

The range of colors of ripening fruit and the cool, shadowy interiors between them caught my eye and offered up the subject for *Loquat Cascade*. I wanted to capture the slightly fuzzy texture of the fruits and contrast it with the thick, leathery leaves. I was able to achieve this by painting each fruit wet-in-wet, lifting out lights, and then dropping in darker tones. Leaves were painted on dry paper, saving the lights and washing away edges to render the corrugations and veins. The interplay of colors was enriched by the light's wide range of reflection. Cool shadows were glazed on and exaggerated to play up every nuance of color essential in capturing the sense of fruit ripening in the California sun.

FREDERICK KUBITZ
Sailboat in Fog–Damariscove Island, ME
22" x 30" (56 cm x 76 cm)
Arches 300 lb. cold press

Bold value changes and subtle colors were used to bring out the numerous effects of the subject, which include top-lighting produced by fog-filtered sunlight, and shadows created by a random shaft of direct sunlight. The darkest values were achieved by layering a series of four washes of French ultramarine mixed with raw umber (to modulate the tone). After a wet-in-wet mixture of veridan and permanent rose, cobalt blue was applied to produce a cool, gray, foggy background. The boats, sails, and buildings were masked. Predominantly cool colors were enhanced by light washes on the sail and roofs and dark, warm tones inside the boats.

PATRICIA REYNOLDS
Champlain Valley Patchwork
31" x 41" (79 cm x 104 cm)
Arches 260 lb. cold press

An underlyimg wash of cobalt blue permeates the painting and conveys the cold colors of the winter. I began wet-in-wet, preserving the whites for contrast and drama. I represented Lake Champlain, the foreground valley, and the Vermont mountains across the lake abstractly to give the look of a winter evening. After letting the work dry, I applied thin glazes with a 4-inch wash brush to create the abstract pattern and dimension in shadow-like forms. Glazed patches of color created the feeling of ice, and warm tones in the foreground allowed the cooler areas to recede and establish the proper perspective.

JIM PITTMAN
Wall Marks
30" x 22" (76 cm x 56 cm)
Strathmore Aquarius
Watercolor with acrylic, pencil,
and crayon

Focusing on shapes and color
movement, both light to dark and
warm to cool, I first laid broad
washes of primary color in mid- to
light-tones, and then began layering
mixed watermedia in a put-and-take
approach. Searching for marks that
indicated the passage of time and
man, I used several techniques until
a depth of surface produced lyrical,
poetic passages. Some marks are
suggestive of ancient times, while
others suggested the graffiti of the
present day.

JANET LAIRD-LAGASSEE
Pumpkins No. 22
15" x 16" (38 cm x 40 cm)
Arches 140 lb. cold press

Using color as the essential tool
for defining the illusion of form,
substance, vitality, and environment,
Pumpkins No. 22 is an exploration
of the color and tonality that forms
compositional relationships. A seem-
ingly limited palette was broadened
to produce numerous variations that
were further enhanced by reflected
and refracted color. Color was altered
and extended through closely graded
glazes to create the impression of
the pumpkins' solid presence.

LOLA JURIS
Lily Legacy
22.5" x 18" (57 cm x 48 cm)
Arches 140 lb. cold press
Watercolor with ink

Lily Legacy deals with the dichotomy of a scene that is simultaneously exciting and tranquil. The challenge was met by counterpointing the long, slow, quiet shadows of the lower portion with the sharp, dark, upper background. Further, the cool-blue upper area changes to a warm yellow-orange below, and this use of a complementary color scheme augments the drama of the image. Some cool color is charged into the warm shadows, color-connecting the two portions of the painting.

LOLA JURIS
Languid Lilies
27" x 20" (69 cm x 51 cm)
Arches 140 lb. cold press
Watercolor with colored pencil

I paint the calla lilies that grow in a small pool on my patio once a year as an ongoing series. In the late afternoon, long shadows play into the scene and create abstract patterns that counter the realism of the subject. The stately serenity of the white lilies, surrounded by a busy tangle of yellow-green leaves, is further dramatized by the stark background. Touches of colored pencil were selectively added to augment various features and rhythmically move the viewer's eye through the painting.

JAN UPP
Aix Marks the Spot
20" x 20" (51 cm x 51 cm)
Arches 140 lb. cold press

The deep contrast of light and
shadow and the low angle of
perspective attracted me to this
subject. I began by gradually
transferring a full-size sketch to
watercolor paper, starting with
the areas of the paper I wanted to
remain unpainted. A yellow wash
was applied everywhere else,
followed by layers of yellow, red,
and blue to gradually build up the
desired values, leaving the small
details until the end.

JAN UPP
Dine In or Take Out
20" x 28" (51 cm x 71 cm)
Arches 140 lb. cold press

The many different shades of white caused by the reflections on the box sides attracted me to this subject. The subtle colors were achieved by first applying many layers of pale washes of aureolin yellow and then permanent rose, followed by Prussian blue, repeating the process until the desired color and value were achieved. When one side of a box needed to be a little darker, I applied three more washes on it, one of each primary color; resulting in some areas having as many as fifteen washes. I layered washes rather than mixing the colors because it produces a richer surface variation.

GERTRUDE LACY
Key West
15" x 22" (38 cm x 56 cm)
Arches 140 lb. cold press

While the sun weakens color, intense darks appear in the shade. I began with random blocks of high-key warm and cool staining colors and painted wet-in-wet, leaving an area near the center untouched. After drying, I painted many of the forms negatively, surrounding them with grayed washes of complementary colors. Darker washes in the shadow areas were added, and some calligraphy defined the forms and gave color to the painting.

CHARLOTTE BRITTON
Above Calistoga
22" x 28" (56 cm x 71 cm)
Arches 300 lb. rough

The intense colors of *Above Calistoga* convey a feeling of the warmth of the sun on a California vineyard in early autumn. Painting the sky a warm violet further heightened the feeling of heat. Working in watercolor on rough paper, I use color to establish the warmth of the subject.

SHARON HILDEBRAND
Space and Illusion
48" x 36" (122 cm x 91 cm)
Fabriano Classico 280 lb. cold press
Watercolor with gold leaf and
Marble Thix

Space and Illusion reflects my strong interest in Oriental art and the symbolism inherent to it. The central koi fish is a prized Sancho Sanshoku, noted for the red blotch on its head and its distinct black-and-white markings. I used gold-leaf paint on the backs and feet of the dragons, symbols of nobility and strength. Darks in the upper right and subtle use of complementary colors lend drama to the composition. The tile color creates a marbled effect, painted wet-in-wet with mostly darks and just touches of greens and pinks.

LORRAINE DENZLER
July
23" x 30" (58 cm x 76 cm)
300 lb. hot press
Watercolor with gouache

In painting *July*, I used gouache for the purity of color it provides me. This approach presents a challenge since definition of objects is by use of color rather than value. Colors must agree with those around them and must integrate composition, space, and movement for the work to be successful.

YVONNE WOOD
Glass and Brass Still Life
23" x 29" (58 cm x 74 cm)
Strathmore bristol plate surface

My still life was set up in front of a window to capture the way sunlight shines on the objects. A white background, transparent bottles, and a lace cloth were chosen for their airiness, and the lace's pattern adds an intricate, abstract design. The paper's plate finish allowed vivid colors to run together and stay on the surface, creating colorful abstract patterns. The plaid cloth and colored bottles are reflected in the brass pot, with each reflection painted into tiny pieces to relate to the next object. The dominant presence of red creates a rhythm throughout the painting that brings unity to the work.

YVONNE WOOD
Musical Instruments Still Life
23" x 29" (58 cm x 74 cm)
Strathmore bristol plate surface

Musical instruments, interlocking and positioned in a triangle, set a rhythmic mood and establish the primary focus of *Musical Instruments Still Life*. Light and shadows cast various patterned forms on the objects. Because of the straight lines of the instruments, I chose striped fabric to give balance to the composition. Lace cloths bring a subtle design and give balance to the white vase on the opposite side. Secondary colors were repeated throughout the painting and color nuances pop in and out. The plate finish of the paper allowed the vibrant colors to stray on the surface.

JORGE BOWENFORBÉS
Mending Sails
22" x 30" (56 cm x 76 cm)
Arches 140 lb. cold press

Every artist has a personal way of seeing and interpreting things in terms of dynamic energy, composition, and shapes. Nowhere in this process is the criteria more manifest than in the use of color. The integration of warm and cool colors present a division of depth and space, besides expressing mood and increasing the emotional impact to the highest level. Since my work is experimental, I have the opportunity to use stronger color contrasts. In *Mending Sails*, the cool, restless aquatic background is enhanced by the warm foreground activity.

MICKEY DANIELS
Yesterday's Antiques
30" x 22" (76 cm x 56 cm)
Arches 140 lb. cold press

I started by preparing a contour drawing of the subject matter and then developed the internal design of each object using a variety of horizontal shapes. Because the theme was recollection of things of the past, orange was chosen as the dominant color to create a warm, nostalgic mood. Each horizontal shape was dampened and floated with color, some with bold, sharp edges, and others with a gentle transition to neighboring white areas. These white areas were left free of masking fluid to allow for freedom of movement. Additional glazes highlight the design structure of the painting and add impact.

CELIA CLARK
The Rejection
24" x 32" (61 cm x 81 cm)
Arches 140 lb. cold press

Though I usually choose a subject for its color, sometimes, such as in *The Rejection*, the subject comes first and I then determine how color can best express it. In this work, color was used to command attention and dramatize the subject: brilliant red was chosen for the anger and frustration it suggests. I chose warm colors over somber colors to imply that a rejection need not be devastating. For richness and vibrancy, I used lightfast colors and mixed them directly on the paper, beginning with washes to set the tone, then building on these with layering.

CHRISTINE M. UNWIN
Moon Rise—Out West
22" x 30" (56 cm x 76 cm)
Arches 140 lb. cold press

Instead of playing single notes of color, I like to paint chords of color because of the many subtle variations it creates. Color is a personal expression: I don't feel limited to paint only local color, I am free to develop colors according to my mood. Color experiments are a continuous process throughout an artist's life, and I try to surprise the viewer with my choice of colors. I love to use bits of pure color right out of the tube as an accent, with these jewel tones proving especially effective when used against neutral, muted colors.

DAVID MADDERN
Cereus in Moonlight
22" x 30" (56 cm x 76 cm)
Arches 300 lb. cold press

The cereus blooms only after nightfall and closes with the first light of dawn. Its extreme delicacy and fragrance permeates the red-black Florida nights. Having studied music, I try to apply music principles to the realization of a painting, besides emotion and intuition. After laying a pale, graded transparent wash, I drew the cereus. The feeling of form, color temperature, melodic themes, and fragmented motifs evolved as I painted. Positive light shapes were glazed with non-staining colors, while the darker negative areas were mainly Winsor green, carmine, and Antwerp blue, mixed directly on the damp paper.

GEORGE W. KLEOPFER, JR.
Thar's Green in Them Thar Hills
16.5" x 32.5" (42 cm x 83 cm)
Double thick illustration board
Watercolor with acrylic

Having driven by this scene many times, never before had I seen it clothed in such uncharacteristic brilliant shades of green. An unusual amount of rain brought a seldom-seen freshness to the color of the landscape. Color became the basis of this painting in order to capture the essence of the scene. Extreme value changes made possible the feeling of spatial distance. I worked with acrylics to achieve many effects otherwise unattainable with gouache.

JOANNA MERSEREAU
Canyon Glory
11" x 15" (28 cm x 38 cm)
Arches 300 lb. cold press

I think in terms of color and how it can be used to most effectively dramatize a subject. In *Canyon Glory*, I used a spotlight effect in which the canyon is bathed in warm color, accentuated by the cool foreground tree and rocky ground. The painting was created by applying glazes of transparent watercolor, using deeper, saturated colors in the foreground.

DELDA SKINNER
Dialogue
26" x 20" (66 cm x 51 cm)
Crescent 110 illustration board
Watercolor with acrylic and pencil

Dialogue is about communication
between all cultures, with color
serving as the universal link
between them. I have developed
my own alphabet and symbols
and use them in hand-carved
stamps with the emphasis on color.
By using watercolor and acrylic
paints, I get a clarity of color that
is unequaled in other mediums.
Layering colors achieves many
variations, hues, tints, and values
that cannot be painted in any
other way.

LINDA S. GUNN
The Pan
22" x 15" (56 cm x 38 cm)
300 lb. hot press
Watercolor with liquid acrylic ink

The Pan was taken from photographs and sketchbook notations I had taken of the Peter Pan statue in London. Contrasting color adds drama and leads the viewer into the painting. The yellow light casts a warm glow on the statue and creates a striking contrast with the deep blue sky. The use of red in key areas of the statue adds warmth not found in the original photograph.

DOUG LEW
The Blue Door
13" x 20" (33 cm x 51 cm)
Arches 140 lb.

My primary intention was to make the white of the door frame and pillars be the focal point of the painting. Though the door is actually black, I felt the need to give it a muted cool color since the shadows that define the door frame were on the cool side. I decided to let one side of the painting be softer than the other to break the severe symmetry of the composition. Sharper, darker treatment of the trees to the right added depth to the doorway.

JOYCE F. PATRICK
Brilliant Passage
22" x 15" (56 cm x 38 cm)
Arches 140 lb. hot press
Watercolor with acrylic and gesso

I find abstract painting to be the
most challenging and satisfying,
with composition central to its
unique methodology. Using several
layers of glazes, I can achieve varying effects and unify one passage
with another. An opaque underpainting interspersed among the glazes
adds form to the composition while
complementary colors create impact
and cause contiguous passages to
intensify each other.

HARRIET MARSHALL GOODE
Delta with Red Hair
28" x 22" (71 cm x 56 cm)
Strathmore Aquarius II
Watercolor with acrylic

I prefer to use colors to accentuate a subject rather than dominate it. For instance, the model for this painting actually has black hair. To keep the picture plane flat, I painted across the lines of my initial drawing with color, integrating background and foreground, then re-established some shapes with the use of line.

JANE FREY
West Light
32" x 45" (81 cm x 114 cm)
Arches double elephant 555 lb.
cold press

West Light represents my appreciation of rich, full color. Putting a wide variety of color in one painting results in complex relationships that work as a whole; in this work, a colorful piece of fabric dictates the selection of other objects used. By using a strong light source, I am free to use vibrant color in the shadows. I wet one small area at a time, drop in local and complementary colors, and allow them to mix on the paper. By combining rich color, unusual combinations of subject matter, and several different dimensions in one composition, I seek to achieve a unique look to my work.

ALLISON CHRISTIE
Bamboo IV
21.5" x 28.5" (55 cm x 72 cm)
Arches 300 lb. cold press

This yellow bamboo, indigenous to Indonesia, undergoes subtle color changes as it ages—from the moss green and burnt sienna of its dried outer husking, to a hot Naples yellow of maturity, and a pale ash white of decay after flowering. Needing to separate the stalks, I created the midground of dark silhouettes with French ultramarine and burnt sienna and the background with greens and bright blue. After finishing the cast shadows, I needed to heighten the husks and bring them forward. These hot spots were achieved with a wash of Dr. Martin's cadmium and rose carthame.

ROBERT S. OLIVER
Vietnamese Boats
14" x 20" (36 cm x 51 cm)
Arches 140 lb. rough

Color relationships and value changes are paramount in my work, with composition and other elements also being of great importance. I derive most of my subject matter from my various travels around the world. Color abounds in the landscape of Vietnam and is echoed in the people and their way of life. The boats pictured are their life and livelihood.

GERALDINE GREENE
Haitian Boat Rudder
16.5" x 25" (42 cm x 64 cm)
Arches 300 lb.

Since I am surrounded by color on the Florida Keys, my subject matter is often dictated by the intensity of color, sunlight, and shadow near my waterfront home. *Haitian Boat Rudder* was painted for its social and historical value as well as the earth colors of the hand-chiseled rudder. After masking the rudder and ropes, I tilted the painting and applied a very thin mixture of alizarin crimson and viridian with a wide brush. I continued the glazes, drying each application with a hair dryer, until the hull was defined along with the partly submerged, but still visible, portion of the rudder.

DEDE COOVER
Serendipity
26" x 26" (66 cm x 66 cm)
Arches watercolor board
Watercolor with acrylic ink

As an abstract artist, I love color and use it as a visual catalyst to create excitement, harmony, and design. I add layers of acrylic ink over the base of watercolor to create a depth of color and movement much like the brilliance of beautiful silks.

JAMES L. KOEVENIG
Orin the Wise: The Philosopher
10.5" x 14.5" (27 cm x 37 cm)
Arches 140 lb. cold press

Many of my paintings focus on people with interesting qualities. This subject is a favorite relative who was expounding on a weighty topic as the late afternoon sun streamed through a skylight. Chiaroscuro was suggested because of the strong illumination with dark shadows on the subject disappearing into the background. Traditional colors were replaced with bright transparent blues, reds, yellows, and purples painted and mixed directly on moistened paper. Details in the background were only suggested and highlights were modified to form interesting shapes and balance the work.

MARSHA GEGERSON
Irreconcilable Differences II
28" x 20" (71 cm x 51 cm)
Winsor and Newton 140 lb. cold press

I have been experimenting with the Oriental concept of using shape and value to create the sense of space within a painting, either by working with a split complementary color scheme or a basic primary triad. In this painting I used the three primaries with an occasional bit of violet. The challenge of this particular color choice was to be constantly aware of which color values and temperatures caused the spaces to recede and which ones brought the shapes forward. I also needed to constantly check to see if all the planes held together, and I found that planning color repetitions helped me accomplish this.

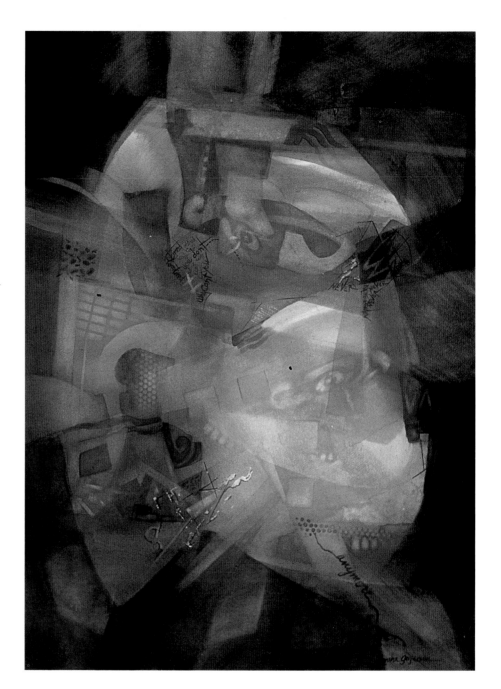

TODD CHALK
Ultimate Spaces I
30" x 36" (76 cm x 91 cm)
Strathmore Aquarius II
Watercolor with acrylic

Color gives this painting its spacious, airy feeling but still keeps its structure. Paint was laid down with paper towels and plastic wrap, stamped with paper, partly painted out then restated with white over color, working back and forth. The resulting pattern of colors play off of each other. I find this painting technique very satisfying.

TODD CHALK
Mountain Scape I
30" x 36" (76 cm x 91 cm)
Strathmore Aquarious II
Watercolor with acrylic and pencil

Mountain Scape I uses minimal color; the drawing carries the visual emphasis of the work. Continually stating and restating patterns, I worked overlays back and forth from medium darks to lights, drawing into the image and leaving and losing shapes as the painting progressed. The dark green was included to balance the whites and give the desired fresh spring-like appearance.

JUDITH KLAUSENSTOCK
Asian Pears
17" x 23" (43 cm x 58 cm)
Arches 140 lb. cold press

My subject matter was chosen for its familiarity, shape, and color, and was generally painted using simple formats. With transparent watercolor enabling the washing-off process, the painting was immersed in water and gently caressed to remove unwanted color, leaving a ghosted image over which many glazes were applied. Shadows helped to make *Asian Pears* unique and interesting.

HENRY DIXON
Night Vision IV–Tablerock Lake
18" x 24.5" (46 cm x 62 cm)
Fabriano 140 lb.

Preferring Winsor and Newton watercolors with a good grade of watercolor paper, my favorite subjects are children and elderly people, old Victorian architecture, and landscapes. I usually photograph my subject matter using slides rather than prints because slides retain the subject's vivid colors. In this painting, I wanted the fountain to stand out against the blackness of the night and give it life.

FRANCES H. McILVAIN
Tropical Island
18" x 22" (46 cm x 56 cm)
Arches 180 lb. cold press
Watercolor with gouache and collage

Rather than producing safe, realistic landscapes, I had the opportunity to try some experimental techniques in which expressing emotions and feelings became the primary challenge. New shapes and forms of foliage in Florida were the inspiration for *Tropical Island*. Pieces of a softly patterned gift bag were collaged to create the land masses. White gouache thinned to a cream-like consistency was allowed to seep through tissues, forming additional patterns and creating a feeling of mystery. Watercolor was applied to make the painting read as a landscape.

JOYCE H. KAMIKURA
Europa
22" x 30" (56 cm x 76 cm)
Lanaquarelle 140 lb. hot press
Watercolor with acrylic

Antiquity associated with old Europe was captured by painting thin layers of transparent reds and blues, layer upon layer, to convey the idea of the aging apparent in old building materials. Finishing layers in Indian red, cadmium red, burnt sienna, and raw umber gave additional warmth. While still wet, I sprayed the painting with water, rolled it with crumpled tissue, and wiped it with toilet rolls. Some sections were lifted by scrubbing with rubbing alcohol to simulate the texture of very old objects. Hot-press paper works best for encouraging the interactions of layered colors.

JANE TALLEY
Creekside
30" x 22" (76 cm x 56 cm)
Strathmore Aquarius 80 lb.
Watercolor with acrylic, ink, and collage

Providing an optical center and dynamic value, color is a major feature of *Creekside*. A limited color palette was selected to elicit an emotional response for the viewer and light and color were organized in toned blocks and balanced with line and texture. I started by applying diluted inks with a spray mister. After drying, wet-in-wet transparent watercolor was used to define the landscape. Accents of drybrushed acrylics and collage were added for texture.

ELAINE WEINER-REED
Awakening
19" x 15" (48 cm x 38 cm)
Arches 140 lb. cold press

Because my technique depended on a wet-in-wet application of color, I wet the entire surface of the paper before applying subsequent washes of new gamboge, quinacridone rose, and ultramarine blue. Gradually, I added the earth colors and some opaques, leaving a dusty warmth of colors. I continued working with new gamboge, Holbein turquoise, and Grumbacher yellow-green to complete the work.

DONNE BITNER
Dance Macabre
30" x 22" (76 cm x 56 cm)
Aquarius II 90 lb. cold press
Watercolor with acrylic and watercolor
crayon

In *Dance Macabre*, I wanted to capture the drama of a performance on stage. Thin layers of acrylic were washed on and textured to create depth and dark, rich color that provided an unusual quality similar to an aged patina. There is a magical feeling to the colors on and around the stage when the dark gives way to light and spectacle.

GLORIA PATERSON
The Orange Belt
22" x 30" (56 cm x 76 cm)
Arches 300 lb. cold press

Executed in a deliberately childlike style, *The Orange Belt* utilizes color choices that suggest the bright heat of Florida. The color is saturated and flat with primary and secondary colors appearing with their complements—the violet palm trees against a yellow field and blue water next to an orange field. The emphasis on simple elements continues in the circular yellow sun, and the exaggerated sun rays carry the viewer's eye around the painting. The circular composition of land carries the viewer's eye deep into space, and the sky was washed with indigo to establish a neutral element.

DAN BURT
Mexicoscape
30" x 22" (76cm x 56cm)
Arches 140lb. cold press

I use color to excite the viewers' eye, stimulate the imagination, and hold interest in the picture. Some of the pigments used in this painting were high chroma (intense), some were granulated and textural, some were subdued so they would enhance the high-chroma colors, and still others were somber tones that complemented the intense colors. I kept the shadows transparent and dark, moving them around the saved white shapes in the composition. After painting one large shadow area, I dropped other dark colors into the wet paint to add variety and spontaneity to the picture.

MICHAEL L. NICHOLSON
Piebald's Vista
14" x 17" (36 cm x 43.2 cm)
Bristol 2-ply board
Watercolor and acrylic

The coolness of the night is still evident in the saturated colors of the waning blue-purple shadows that are juxtaposed with the radiant illumination that backlights the composition. The local color of a red-earth prairie is transformed into atmospheric color of richness and depth with an organization of hue, value, and intensity. The versatility, strength, and permanence of saturated acrylics allowed me to create the initial plein air sketch and to complete the work in the studio.

WAYNE H. SKYLER
Chinatown
22" x 28" (56 cm x 71 cm)
Arches watercolor board rough

As a realist painter, color plays an important role in the creative process by setting the mood for the image. The inspiration for *Chinatown* was the wide array of brilliant colors and shapes that are unique to this part of the city, capturing an early-morning sun casting strong shadow patterns across the vibrant mix of colors and shapes. The sunlight, mingling warm colors, cool shadows, and cast geometric patterns, transforms a flat, ordinary street scene into an exciting combination of color, shadow, and texture.

NORDIA KAY
Summer's Bounty
22" x 30" (56 cm x 76 cm)
Arches 140 lb. cold press

The color balance of *Summer's Bounty* began with initial planned color washes onto a wet surface. At this point, the painting already had color design, mood, and movement, and this set the tone of the work. Most of the strong contrasts of light and dark were kept in the foreground; I tried to show perspective through the softer, paler colors with broken details in the background.

MARGARET M. MARTIN
Entree to Elegance
17.5" x 21.5" (45 cm x 55 cm)
Arches 300 lb. cold press

Color can create temperature, mood, and mystery and it is inextricably linked with value—every color has a value, and every value has a color. The vitality of color and the vibrancy of contrast were achieved by working out value relationships at the start. Warm violet shadows complement the pale yellow light areas. A limited subdued palette was used, layering thin color washes to keep a transparency and glowing color.

MARY SORROWS HUGHES
Coastal Rose Hips—Maine Surprise
22" x 30" (56 cm x 76 cm)
Arches 300 lb. cold press

I am stimulated by vivid dramatic color and subjects that are unusual and surprising. Watercolor is my preferred medium due to its fluid, sweeping quality and its propensity toward happy accidents and unexpected results. Salt was thrown into areas of wet paint to create texture on the rose hips, and layers of color were built up to portray the vivid green of the leaves and the red of the rose hips. Blues were later dropped into areas of the leaves. The complementary nature of the greens and reds helped heighten the visual effect of each, which added to the power of the painting's color statement.

ANN PEMBER
Peony Unfurled
21" x 29" (53 cm x 74 cm)
Saunders Waterford 140 lb. cold press

Subtle color changes that occur over flower petals intrigue me. Colors can be wonderfully clean as well as lush, and are even reflected from surrounding objects. Using transparent pigments for clean, luminous results, I applied colors to wet areas and let them mingle on the paper. Complementary colors, such as the blue and orange in the petals, make the painting lively and vibrant.

KAREN MATHIS
Vacation Stop
22" x 25" (56 cm x 64 cm)
Arches 140 lb. cold press
Watercolor with gouache

I wanted to use colors that made the subject and light around her glow. The complementary combination of crisp yellow against the more neutral violet accomplished that goal. Touches of yellow gouache were added in the violet to soften the shadows cast from the tree above and to unify the background with the yellow of the chairs. The unusual color combination might surprise viewers and draw them in for closer inspection.

JANE R. HOFSTETTER
Emergence
21" x 29" (53 cm x 74 cm)
Strathmore 5-ply illustration board
Watercolor with acrylic

Dramatizing a tiny cluster of leaves, berries, and small white flowers presented a difficult challenge. Beginning with transparent watercolor washes of warm bright colors, I added warm and cool darks for contrast. Washes of pale acrylic in various areas gave a veiled look to the underpainting, and the subject was defined using energetic calligraphic brushstrokes. A final check made sure each piece of the subject was similar yet unique. The warm transparent color from the background gives *Emergence* much of its dramatic glow.

BENJAMIN MAU
Wind Dusk
40" x 30" (102 cm x 76 cm)
Arches 140 lb. cold press

Wind Dusk was first designed on wet paper to allow the natural flow of background watercolor to be part of the creative process. Naples yellow, burnt umber, and Prussian blue were used as the primary colors, with salt and sawdust applied for texture. Additional layers of color with touches of magenta and alizarin crimson were built up, the layering creating a rich and complex visual impact. The house and flowers were drybrushed to complete the work.

JANE E. JONES
Musical Mesa
22" x 30" (56 cm x 76 cm)
Arches 140 lb. cold press

Musical Mesa is a composition based my reaction to classical music; the music evokes different hues, color temperatures, and intensities. I began by drawing horizontal shapes when suddenly a clash of symbols created vertical shapes for conflict, which then led to a landscape. Painting wet-in-wet using gradation of hue, color temperature, value, and intensity creates visual movement. The light meets the dark yet the painting maintains a sense of unity.

KATHLEEN JARDINE
Sacred and Profane Love: The
Copulations of Monsters
48" x 51" (122 cm x 130 cm)
Lanaquarelle #1114 hot press

Although I work only from life, all of
my work employs intensified colors
that are used to elicit what might be
called hallucinatory realism. My
paintings are allegories that com-
press detail for layered meaning. I
have no strategy for making them;
I just work as if in a spell.

CARMEN NEWMAN BAMMERT
Water's Edge
20" x 28" (51 cm x 71 cm)
Winsor Newton 260 lb. cold press
Watercolor with white ink

I floated a triad of peacock blue, new gamboge, and a mixture of opera and rose madden on wet paper. As the colors mingled, they produced organic shapes, textures, and secondary hues. After drying, I studied the work for a sense of subject and found a wing-like shape in the saved white area and outlines of leaves and branches. I then began to develop the concept of a snow goose landing along a stream. Darks were achieved by adding thalo blue and alizarin crimson. By using a limited palette, I maintained a fresh look, and the colors gave the painting a mystical, airy feeling.

RAKA BOSE SAHA
Prelude
30" x 22" (76 cm x 56 cm)
Arches 300 lb. cold press
Watercolor with acrylic and ink

Color and composition are interlaced and are the most important elements of my work. I do not distort forms, but I enjoy unrealistic colors because they give my paintings an abstract quality. After applying the main body of colors with acrylics, I covered the entire painting with water-based black ink. When the paper was dry, I soaked it in cold water and washed it with a soft sponge. This caused the ink on top of the paint to wash away, leaving ink embedded in the tiny crevices of the paper. I accentuated various areas with more acrylics to complete the work.

NEDRA TORNAY
Oia, Santorini
29" x 20" (74 cm x 51 cm)
Arches 300 lb. rough
Watercolor with acrylic, gouache,
and gesso

When my transparent watercolor
wasn't producing the desired
effects, I employed other techniques
to make it work. I applied gesso,
then painted with transparent watercolor. White acrylic was used in thin
washes to lighten values, and small
sunlit plants were rendered with
bright opaque gouache because
complementary colors in minute
areas appear dull. With transparent
watercolor I juxtaposed complements to achieve brilliance, then
used complementary colors as
glazes to dull and darken values.
Due to the intense California sunlight, the buildings could have been
portrayed as being white, but I feel
my colors bring more dimension
and interest to a familiar subject.

MARILYN GROSS
Urban Promise
22" x 30" (56 cm x 76 cm)
Arches 140 lb. hot press
Watercolor with acrylic, ink, gesso,
and Caran d'ache

Color is perhaps the most powerful communication tool an artist has, since color seems to speak directly to the soul of the viewer. In *Urban Promise*, I have used color to convey the feeling of rural areas versus urban areas, using large simple areas of earth tones to represent rural areas, and more sophisticated violets and blues to indicate approaching urban areas. Smooth open spaces representing rural areas are in quiet contrast to the more active portion representing urban life, not only in color but also in texture and line.

ROBERT LAMELL
Saltillo Cathedral
22" x 30" (56 cm x 76 cm)
Arches 140 lb. cold press

Late-afternoon sun casts warm rays of color mixed with spots of highlight on the front of the cathedral, reflecting up from the lit foreground. A play of warm hues, balanced by cool complements, lead into the portal with a glow of color. The light at the cathedral entrance anticipates the drama one would experience on entering the building, directing and drawing the viewer into an expected mystery. *Saltillo Cathedral* was done all at once, capturing the light as it reflected off the textured wood, setting up a contrast on the marble architectural elements.

MILES G. BATT, SR.
Left-Handed Complement
17" x 23" (43 cm x 58 cm)
Arches 140 lb. hot press

The intent of *Left-Handed Complement* is to present an image that defies closure—is it a seascape or an envelope? Ocean, sky, and water are modified by changing sunlight and warm color vibrations that are produced by light on surfaces and by the atmosphere at various times of the day. Full sheet washes were applied with an Oriental Hake brush, followed by countless airbrush glazes to blend the surface with subtle color nuances. Using frisket paper for masking, the cool shadow under the envelope flap was airbrushed. Finally the buttons and string were carefully rendered with a brush.

BARBARA GEORGE CAIN
The Blues Club
22" x 30" (56 cm x 76 cm)
Arches 140 lb. cold press
Watercolor and gesso

The warm skin tones of the musicians performing at the annual art festival in Fort Worth, Texas were the inspiration for the warm colors of *The Blues Club*. For contrast, a wide range of cool hues, values, and intensities was used: blue grays, violets, darker and brighter blues to blue greens. To draw attention to the face of the larger figure, I applied the most intense color and greatest contrast. After painting the larger figures, piano, and background, I layered diluted white gesso over the background and loosely painted the other figures and musical instruments.

EVALYN J. DYER
Sunflower Symphony
22" x 30" (56 cm x 76 cm)
Whatman 200 lb. cold press

As part of the artistic license available to painters, my color choice is based on my emotion rather than on the actual color of the subject matter. *Sunflower Symphony* reflects my love of blues and purples. A sense of spiritual serenity is projected by the interaction of the many soft hues and darker accents which complement the analogous colors. After an initial wet-in-wet application of large areas of color to establish the dominant color theme, glazing was used to build up form with lights and darks. Brush spattering added texture and darker accents added sparkle.

PAUL W. NIEMIEC, JR.
Black Forest
17" x 19" (43 cm x 48 cm)
Arches 140 lb. cold press

When designing my paintings, I use color relationships as a means of pursuing unity and balance. I favor a tonal approach, using grayed colors, shades, and tints, with restrained use of saturated color accents, placing emphasis upon atmospheric effects of light. For this portrait of my daughter, a dark warm background was used as a foil to focus attention on her eyes and whimsical gaze. Color harmony and richness were developed through the use of a limited palette, gradation of color values and saturation, analogous and complementary colors, and dark accents to enliven nearby colors.

RICHARD SEDDON
The Diablerets Near Sion,
Switzerland
19.5" x 19.5" (50 cm x 50 cm)
unpressed handmade paper
Watercolor with India ink and pencil

One feature of the light on a cloudy day in the Swiss Alps is the way the rectilinear forms of the ice-covered high rocks attain a pearlescent quality. The higher the gaze travels upward the more this effect is seen, until the very high slopes lose their tints and become monochrome, devoid of color. At this level, they blend into the sky until one cannot tell where mountains end and sky begins. As the gaze descends, color increases, and at the tree line, full color reigns and everything is quite distinct.

JANET SHAFFER
Crescendo
22" x 28" (56 cm x 71 cm)
Illustration board
Watercolor with acrylic

I was motivated to paint *Crescendo* after traveling in the Southwest, where I was intrigued by the colors, the open expanses, the brilliant skies, and the transcendent light on trees and land. I chose illustration board because of its stability and the way it allows a loosely rendered, somewhat abstract look. The board also tolerates additions of texture, which helped the glazes to create living color. To emphasize the push and pull of contrasting darks and lights, I applied successive layers of water-diluted color over certain areas of the trees, sky, and earth masses.

MARILYN SEARS BOURBON
Santorini I
14.5" x 21.5" (37 cm x 55 cm)
Arches 140 lb. hot press
Watercolor with gouache and
watercolor pencils

The Greek village of Santorini is perched amidst cliffs and dramatic verticals on the edge of a volcanic bay. I flattened the three-dimensional conflict of buildings and rocks into a textured tapestry of alternating blues, whites, and local color. On top of transparent color washes, I built layers of gouache, which I applied, scraped out, and sponged into lines and shapes to form positive and negative space. Watercolor pencils enhanced lines and built color contrasts.

J. LURAY SCHAFFNER
A Different Freedom
30" x 20" (76 cm x 51 cm)
4-ply museum board
Watercolor with ink, gouache, pencil,
and collage

Composing this painting on black
museum board was a new experience for me, and I went through a
process of applying a number of
different papers, inks, and paints to
alter the board's black surface. No
matter what surface I'm working
on, I keep in mind that color and
value are relative concepts and
depend completely on what is
around them. As a composition
develops, I find special satisfaction
in finding a bright center of interest
in most of my work as well as giving
the viewer other areas to seek out
and enjoy.

PAINTING TEXTURE

The importance of texture in all styles of painting is unquestionable. The use of texture is extensive in abstract painting; there are myriad ways of expressing it. In realism, texture is found in the way the brush reacts differently to each object and the space it holds in the painting. Texture is more than merely paint; it's achieved even through the painted surface itself. The varied surfaces—hot press, gessoed, cold press, rough, and extreme rough—add to the finished look of the painting. The surfaces are chosen to best reflect the mood each artist wishes to achieve and the subject or nonsubject that calls for these varied handlings.

Texture can be made up of merely thick and thin paint qualities. Opaque and heavy paints contrast with a thin wash laid quickly over the paper. Applying turpentine to paper before painting adds a different look to the washes placed over it. With such tools as resists, wax or crayon, and salt, a simple wash can have a unique texture. By placing wire mesh or lace on the paper and then running washes over it, a new texture is produced. Painting in cold air achieves a wonderful effect with freezing paint.

The artist's imagination is the most valuable tool in finding texture. There are so many possibilities even in the simple art of scraping paper. Different effects are created merely by changing the scraper: a piece of wood, a credit card, cardboard, and even fingernails. Painters can use stippling with a hard, short-hair bristle brush, dab the paint on with a sponge, or splatter with an old toothbrush. Even watermarks can become advantages and create just the right note to express a subject. Texture can take a dull design and remake it to into an exciting piece of art.

Texture affects not just our sense of sight, but also our sense of touch. A silk surface reflects light, and a rough one absorbs light. When texture is used successfully, the surfaces will look and feel wet or dry, rough or smooth. Even color is affected by texture. The same color may look different when it's washed on or dry-brushed, when it's painted on smooth paper or on rough paper, when it's been scraped, or when any other foreign substance is added to the paint.

Every surface we encounter has texture. We study it in nature: in trees, in crumbling stone walls, in the way water changes the surface of rocks, and in how moss and lichen play upon them. Texture is everywhere. With different methods we try to bring all of this to our paintings. This collection will show the many ways, some obvious and some ever so subtle, in which texture enhances our paintings.

BETTY CARMELL SAVENOR
Out on a Limb
28" x 21" (71 cm x 53 cm)
Strathmore 140 lb. illustration board
Watercolor with watercolor inks

Texture is a necessary component of my work; it brings my painting beyond the two-dimensional by adding density and penetration of color, such as one sees in nature. Starting with a limited palette, I layered my varied-color washes without any preconceived ideas. While still wet, certain areas were textured by spattering, misting, and stamping with anything that produced an unusual surface. Finishing touches included brush-work, lettering, and collage with assorted papers and silk tissue.

ROBERT SAKSON
Secrets
22" x 30" (56 cm x 76 cm)
Arches 140 lb. rough

At Hartung's General Store in Hope, New Jersey, two
small girls just happened to sit down to eat the candy they
had purchased. I wanted to catch the rough texture of the
aging store and chose to mix my colors with Winsor &
Newton Aquapasto watercolor medium, a translucent gel. I
used this mixture primarily in the dark shadow areas to
give them a deep luminescence and lifelike effect.

MARY LOU FERBERT
Thistle and Spalling Bridge
39" x 27.5" (100 cm x 70 cm)
Arches 555 lb. rough

Interpreting the concrete aggregate
of the old Rocky River Bridge was
the technical challenge in executing
this painting. Years of heavy use left
the bridge deteriorated with spalling
exposing some of the substructure.
Unable to find a shortcut method
of interpreting the concrete, I painted
slowly, moving from cool to warm,
to establish the planes of the structure.
Color used in the bridge remained
subdued behind the more brilliantly
painted wild thistle.

ROBERT W. BRAGG
Vicki's Buoys
18" x 24" (46 cm x 61 cm)
Arches 140 lb. cold press

During a vacation in Maine, I
came upon a lobsterman's shed
whose many angles and textures
intrigued me. The softness and
drapery of the old sail contrasted
with the rough line of the silver-
gray shingles and the brightly
painted lobster buoys. Nets, bottles,
harpoons, and other sea mementos
added to the overall interest. I
attribute my ability to recognize
interesting textures and subject
matter to my early art-student
training in realism.

ALEX POWERS

14 Million Children are Living in Poverty

20" x 40" (51 cm x 102 cm)

Strathmore illustration board, plate finish

Watercolor with gouache and charcoal

Texture is the exciting alternative to the grouping and simplifying of shapes. Slick-surface illustration board lends itself well to creating surface variations. Since the heads were not broken up enough to suit me, I forced a loaded brush of white gouache along the top of the painting, causing the gouache to run and further fragment the heads.

PATRICIA REYNOLDS
Moon Series: Acropolis
21.5" x 29.5" (55 cm x 75 cm)
Arches 140 lb. cold press

Texture was used to create interest, contrast, dimension, and to define subjects. In *Moon Series: Acropolis*, the sponged-out areas added to the feeling of crumbling ruins and the surrounding rock masses leading up to the summit of the Acropolis. Dark areas of the painting were broken into an interesting pattern using texture created by dropping color from a brush and spattering, sponging, and misting.

ELAINE WENTWORTH
The Woodlot Trail
20" x 30" (51 cm x 76 cm)
Waterford 300 lb. cold press

The richly textured underbrush in the forest that surrounds the snow-covered footbridge provides the strong contrast in this composition. Diagonals create movement and lead the viewer deep into the woods. Textures were created by drybrushing over washes of warm and cool tones, spattering with a brush, and by scraping dry paint.

PAT FORTUNATO
Material Pleasures #1
22" x 30" (56 cm x 76 cm)
Lanaquarelle 140 lb. cold press

To achieve the desired textural effect of the old, thin, soft fabric and the slick glass required repeated glazes of warm and cool tones. I started with the warm yellowish-pink hue cast on the fabric by the red carnation and when dry, used a cobalt blue wash over that. As many as seven washes of varying hues and values were applied before adding thin darker lines and rubbing out light lines to produce the creases and wrinkles. Lace was carefully painted so as not to overstate its texture and a swirl pattern in the vase created abstract shapes in the reflections.

JIM PITTMAN
Line Dancing
30" x 22" (76 cm x 56 cm)
Strathmore Aquarius
Watercolor with acrylic, watercolor
pencil, and watercolor crayon

Texture is an important element in
my work and was achieved using a
brush and a painting knife, besides
drawing with a water-soluble crayon.
Using Aquarius paper, I started with
large washes and built in layers by
glazing, lifting, scratching, and
scrubbing. I continued using mixed
watermedia in a push-and-pull
method until I was satisfied with the
final image. This work is loosely
based on the idea of walls and the
marks left by time and man, varying
from ancient scratchings to contem-
porary graffiti. Without using short-
cuts, I wanted the act of creation to
be visible from the beginning
washes to the finished painting.

VAUGHN L. JACKSON
Retired But Willing
29" x 21" (74 cm x 53 cm)
Arches 140 lb. rough

Texture and the way light affects texture are important in my work. The scaling paint of the shed door required many glazes and delicate drybrushing to achieve the weathered look. I painted a basic red on the wall and then layered glazes, gradually working until the grain was drybrushed last. Many glazes were built up over the copper horse's basic color to reach the smooth, metallic roundness that contrasts with the door and wall. The loose, wispy grass contributes to the feeling of the horse's movement.

TRUDY M. WHITNEY
Ashram
19" x 24" (48 cm x 61 cm)
Strathmore 300 series 100 lb.
Watercolor with gouache, acrylic,
and ink

Richly textured surfaces, influenced by the ancient surfaces of Ottoman Turkey, added to the creative expression I sought. A layer of torn absorbent material on presoaked paper was partially covered by pouring a thin, creamy gouache that left an imbedded texture. Alternating and drying each layer, watercolor, inks, and acrylics were applied and enhanced by using water, alcohol, and bleach to give the translucent depth of patterning. Textured markings were directly applied to further add to the mystic tone and orientation of the painting.

SHARON HILDEBRAND
Moonlit Garden
33" x 25" (84 cm x 64 cm)
Fabriano Classico 280 lb. cold press
Watercolor with casein

Transparent watercolor was used along with casein and colored pencil to produce the various light and texture effects in *Moonlit Garden*. Thicker and more opaque than watercolor, casein was applied to obtain the look of thick, wavy glass windows, while delicate colored-pencil lines create the screen texture on the windows. Semi-circular halos of light were applied with the bottom of a cup dipped into paint and pressed onto the paper. Texture helped create the mood of a late, dark night with dim, broken light through the windows. The desired result was achieved through the use of a smooth, soft-surface paper that could be lifted easily for soft edges.

GERRY GROUT
Still Life with Horse Skull
22" x 30" (56 cm x 76 cm)
140 lb. hot press
Watercolor with powdered charcoal and
dry pigments

*Collection of Paradise Valley
Community College*

I began by sprinkling powdered charcoal and dry pigment onto the paper and then briefly held it under a shower head. The animal skulls and bones were further defined by surrounding them with watercolor washes that suggest a Southwestern environment. Charcoal-pencil line work added necessary details and completed the painting.

FREDI TADDEUCCI
Windswept
21.25" x 28.25" (54 cm x 73 cm)
Arches 140 lb. cold press
Watercolor with acrylic and colored
pencil

To create texture and movement and add energy and vibrancy to the painting, colors and shapes were randomly applied without thought of a subject. Dropping wrinkled tissue shapes onto wet paint, I rolled with a brayer to produce a broken texture and then added colored pencil. Further texture was created by placing plastic wrap on the wet paint, letting the paint dry, and then pulling away the plastic wrap. To achieve a rich depth of color, rubbing alcohol was scattered on the painting and acrylic paint was layered on top.

DELDA SKINNER
Ancient Joy
20" x 30" (51 cm x 76 cm)
Crescent 100 lb. illustration board
Watercolor with acrylic and watercolor
pencil

Texture helps convey the idea of an archeological discovery; it adds mystery, intrigue, and excitement. Texture not only adds color and spatial depth, but also adds tactile impressions to this work's surface. These effects were achieved by different techniques: many layers of washes, airbrushing, stencils used as overlays, and scratching with various tools. Using hand-carved stamps, I added and lifted up paint in various areas. Flow release and alcohol were sprayed on and rolled off with towels when the paint was partially dry. Finally, fine detailing was added with watercolor pencils.

JACK R. BROUWER
Palamos Blancos
21" x 29" (53 cm x 74 cm)
Arches 300 lb. cold press

Texture is often the one element that is ignored in a successful painting, yet this subtle quality can elevate a painting to a higher level. The dark background of *Palamos Blancos* needed to suggest atmosphere without drawing attention away from the girl or the doves. Using texture to contrast surfaces, I was able to create energy in what could otherwise be considered a dull area. To accomplish this, I concentrated on the texture of the girl's dress, particularly the ruffles and embroidered top. The doves' texture was kept simple, except when showing the in-flight movement of their wings.

ANNE KITTEL
Flotsam and Jetsam No. 6
19" x 22" (48 cm x 56 cm)

The inspiration for the series of paintings that includes *Flotsam and Jetsam No. 6* came from a battered pair of wire-frame eyeglasses I found at a beach-front restaurant. Using textured paper, it was possible to paint smooth washes, such as those used for the seashells, as well as texture (with sedimentary pigments). I used paper towels to lift wet paint, a plastic strawberry basket as a stencil to paint the mesh bag, and sprinkled beach sand in wet areas to capture the appearance of objects found on a beach.

LENA R. MASSARA
One with his Music
24" x 30" (61 cm x 76 cm)
Fabriano 300 lb.
Watercolor with pastels

I worked out the composition for this painting with a pen-and-ink drawing, and then transferred the lines of the drawing onto watercolor paper. After an initial application of watercolor, I began working with both watercolor and pastel to divide the shapes and build texture, and then went over the pastel with washes of watercolor. I continued building up the surface in this way until the painting was finished. The richness and interplay achieved using liquid and dry media allowed me to produce varied strokes and create the near-abstract shapes within the representational theme.

BETTY M. STROPPEL
Up for Overhaul
22" x 30" (56 cm x 76 cm)
Arches 300 lb. cold press

Up for Overhaul, one of a series of paintings of aging boat rudders, presented an opportunity to use texture to portray a weather-worn object. The intimacy of a close-up view accentuated the tactile quality of the subject, and the variety of textural effects maintains viewer interest. To achieve these effects, I used wadded plastic wrap, rubber scrapers, spatulas, spattering, and stamping.

MONROE LEUNG
Cluster of Shapes
16" x 24" (41 cm x 61 cm)
Arches 300 lb. rough

I found the dilapidation and deterioration of the aging buildings to be intriguing subject matter. Weather-beaten wood, peeling plaster, and old mortar provided an ideal opportunity to explore various techniques—wet-in-wet, drybrush, flicking, and scraping. The rough, rundown conditions of the structures made texture one of the most dominant factors in this painting.

JUDITH WENGROVITZ
Baskets
22" x 30" (56 cm x 76 cm)
Arches 300 lb. cold press

Baskets emphasizes the design and texture used in weaving a basket. After a pencil sketch was completed, the highlighted areas were masked and allowed to dry. A light-color glaze was applied over the whole surface, and then a darker color was painted over that. The wet paint was scraped with the beveled edge of an Aquarelle brush to create the basket's weave pattern before the masking was removed. Additional glazes were added to show modeling and shadows. Using these techniques, I was able to achieve a realistic texture in my painting.

SIDNEY T. MOXHAM
Song of Kokopelli
30" x 30" (76 cm x 76 cm)
Strathmore cold press
Watercolor with acrylic, ink, and
crayons

All aspects of my paintings use texture as part of the
whole. In *Song of Kokopelli*, I used clear shelf paper to
block out images I wanted saved and then applied paint
with a wide brush. Many techniques were used to create
the texture—imprinting with paper towels, tissues, frisket,
charcoal, crayons, alcohol, and tracings—all part of the
process necessary to complete the painting.

ANN ZIELINSKI
Whiskey and Old Apples
22" x 30" (56 cm x 76 cm)
Arches 300 lb.
Watercolor with acrylic and crayon

Arising from a series of previous brush-and-ink studies, recreating the texture and aged surface of the whiskey jugs proved to be an all-important facet of this painting. Once committed to memory, the studies were set aside and I began painting. To create the added texture, I took a painting and plastered it randomly with handmade Japanese papers, leaving only some of the original painting exposed. My best paintings are realized by blocking out any preconceived endings and relying instead on memories.

ALINE BARKER
The Robins are Back
22" x 30" (56 cm x 76 cm)
Arches 140 lb. cold press
Watercolor with acrylic, polymer,
and inks

Using a number of techniques, texture can give a painting depth and excitement. After pouring pigments onto dampened paper, I waited for an image to suggest itself, in this case a tree. Much of the texture was created using a variety of watermedia, pouring them onto the dampened surface, and allowing them to react as they merged. The tree was developed using a plastic pot scrubber and salt, which was sprinkled onto the lower-right corner. Further mixing with a spatula added to the texture of the piece.

RICHARD J. SULEA
Wall with Roof
14" x 21" (36 cm x 53 cm)
Arches 300 lb. cold press
Watercolor with gouache

Weathered architectural forms, with their varied surface textures, can be realized by experimenting with a variety of unconventional tools. Working either wet or dry, the surface can be blotted, scratched, and manipulated to create form in light. Most often, paper towels, sponges, sandpaper, and razor blades are employed in the later stages of development.

ROBERT S. OLIVER
Gold Leaf
14" x 14" (36 cm x 36 cm)
Crescent 310 lb. cold press
Watercolor with acrylic, tempera, and modeling paste

The addition of texture through the use of modeling paste in *Gold Leaf* introduced another dimension and added excitement to the painting, both in surface treatment and as in the variety of paint-application techniques. Many transparent glazes of watercolor and acrylic, coupled with opaque applications of tempera, produced the finished painting. The addition of iridescent gold acrylic brought excitement to the painting.

DIANE JACKSON
Rhapsody
28.5" x 18.5" (72 cm x 47 cm)
Arches 300 lb. cold press

When forming ideas for *Rhapsody*, I concentrated on composition and then focused on developing a contrasting blend and harmonious flow of textures. Items in the still life were chosen for their unique beauty, complexity of combined textures, and array of color. I painted the subject life-size and used the white of the paper rather than masking. Details of the painting needed to blend and flow without appearing congested or confused while letting the items retain their individual textural characteristics.

CAROL HUBBARD
Winter Afternoon
29" x 41" (74 cm x 104 cm)
Arches 300 lb. cold press

Texture is not a photographic copy of the surface the artist is trying to paint, but rather a rendition of the color, shape, and value of the particular surface. *Winter Afternoon* relies on the successful rendering of surface texture and life-size subject matter for its impact. I often throw the weathered baskets and pails that I have collected into my courtyard before a snowfall and am usually rewarded with a composition that doesn't look arranged. Simplicity, repeated forms, and a monochromatic palette support the textural quality of the painting.

ZETTA JONES
Aura
30" x 22" (76 cm x 56 cm)
Arches 300 lb. rough
Watercolor with ink

Many of my paintings consist of representational floral designs that incorporate geometric abstracts, with the flowers dictating the design. Arches 300 lb. rough paper has a surface compatible with heavy texture, especially when using watercolor interchangeably with silver ink. The wells of the paper hold many layers of glazes when rendering deep colors, such as in *Aura*. The textured geometrical design of the painting supports the representational iris and enhances it.

JEAN R. NELSON
Cosmic Game
22" x 30" (56 cm x 76 cm)
Lanaquarelle 140 lb. rough
Watercolor with acrylic and gesso

I used texture both as an underlying resist and a modifying overlay, finding the use of a textured resist on unpainted paper gives a more integrated result than anything I could superimpose later. In *Cosmic Game*, I began by printing a word-grid cut in reverse on linoleum. Using haphazard brushstrokes of thinned acrylic matte medium on the block, I then utilized both linoleum and cardboard shapes to print textured areas. The underlying word-grid provided a subtle texture and a sense of mystery, with additional shapes softening the edges and adding dimension.

DONNE BITNER
Flowers for Baylee
30" x 22" (76 cm x 56 cm)
Aquarius II 140 lb. cold press
Watercolor with acrylic and watercolor
crayon

When I begin a painting, my
primary intention is to create a
rich, textured surface. I layer thin
washes of acrylic and mist with
alcohol to lift the paint and reveal
some of the underlying layer. Only
in the last stages does the painting
come together and resolve the
many initial loose ends. In *Flowers
for Baylee*, texture gives the three-
dimensional areas depth and weight
and allows for back-and-forth
movement of space.

MARI M. CONNEEN
Corkboard Architecture
27" x 30" (69 cm x 76 cm)
Strathmore 500 lb. illustration board

I wanted to create an environmental statement using the corkboard as a background. Our natural environment was depicted by painting postage stamps, and older architecture was represented by the renderings hinged together. Objects on the corkboard were masked out and more than thirty washes, from light to dark, were applied with a paint roller. After this process was complete, the mask was removed, and the in-painting began. Edges of the painted pieces of paper were scraped with a razor blade to give them a three-dimensional effect.

RUTH COCKLIN
MEM-114
12.5" x 18.5" (32 cm x 49 cm)
Arches 140 lb. cold press

Trained in architectural illustration, I decided to apply my watercolor skills to portray the luminous effects of reflections. Classic automobiles, with their curvilinear designs, massive chrome grilles, headlights, and bumpers, became my focus. The numerous patterns in the reflection added fascination and complexity to the painting. Layers of glazing over brilliant, white paper gave a stained-glass effect, which I used to soften the lines between images. The design of the painting was kept very defined, clean, and focused.

PEGGY BROWN
Drifting By
34" x 26" (86 cm x 66 cm)
Rives heavyweight
Watercolor with charcoal and graphite
pencil

Various dry media worked wet-in-wet along with transparent watercolor help me achieve the tactile feeling prevalent in my work. Numerous layers of watercolor are supplemented with, and complemented by, powdered charcoal, graphite, colored pencil, or pastels, allowing each to dry completely before continuing. While each stage melds with preceding ones, individual stages still show through to the end and become an integral part of the finished work. The design, with its positive and negative structures tied together with organic lines and washes, is based on my previous semi-abstract paintings of Victorian homes.

MARY C. CHAN
Mary's Catch
30" x 22" (76 cm x 56 cm)
Crescent 300 lb. board smooth

Mary's Catch represents the combined effects of color and texture working together. It is a personal statement about a day of fishing. My goal was to paint the fish as if it had just been caught, still alive and submerged in water. Using watercolor wet-in-wet and masking the bubble and algae areas, I applied dark colors around the fish to give the illusion of the dark side of life, reds for some warmth, and greens and cerulean to depict water. The desired effect was obtained by direct painting in some areas and throwing and flecking the paint in others.

JUDY CASSAB
Desert Night
22" x 30" (57 cm x 76 cm)
Arches
Watercolor with gouache

The subject of *Desert Night* is
the spiritual, surreal landscape of
Rainbow Valley in the center of
Australia. I allowed the thin willow-
charcoal drawing to be visible under
the watercolor to help establish the
painting's texture. Pelican black
gouache accented the forms and
added to the overall textural effect.

GEORGE GIBSON
Caracas Condos
21" x 29" (53 cm x 74 cm)
Arches 300 lb. rough

Constructed from whatever discarded materials were available, the housing common to Caracas, Venezuela interested me with its many textures and colors. I used a drybrush technique in conjunction with sandpaper and razor blade. As a contrast to the rougher building surfaces, I still retained a wash effect in the foliage areas. Varied textures emphasized the array of materials used in creating these structures.

BETTY L. ANGLIN
Impressions of Charleston
11" x 12.5" (28 cm x 32 cm)
Arches 140 lb. cold press
Watercolor with gouache

I use a wax-resist technique developed after experimenting with batik. Working on very absorbent rag watercolor paper, I drew outlines of the shapes in my picture with permanent black ink, and then filled in the shapes with bright color. Once the paint dried, I covered the colored shapes with a melted combination of beeswax and parafin. After the wax mixture cooled, I painted washes of India ink and dark watercolors over the entire painting to fill in the lines between shapes and the small cracks that occur in the wax. When the paper dried, I removed the wax.

SYBIL MOSCHETTI
Buttoned
30" x 40" (76 cm x 102 cm)
Arches 300 lb. rough
Watercolor with pencil

I began *Buttoned* by applying irregular bands and areas of color until the piece became overwhelmingly complex. A large center section was torn out, and the remaining two uneven pieces were torn and reinserted into the open space. This was glued to another sheet of paper and the floating central pieces were attached to the perimeter with sections torn or cut from the leftovers. Multiple pencil lines drawn in a spider-web pattern softened the painting while adding a sense of mystery. Painted buttons were collaged to catch the eye and add a touch of reality.

BETTY C. BOYLE
Peek at the Deep
24" x 30" (61 cm x 76 cm)
Crescent board
Watercolor with gouache and gesso

Having done a carefully rendered tree painting on expensive watercolor board, I decided it was too photographic. Turning it upside down, I layered gesso over the painting, allowing some underlying colors to show through. This effect suggested an underwater scene that I enlarged upon by using a sponge dipped in watercolor and gouache to represent coral and vegetation. The resulting texture helped depict the deep sea and establish realism.

LEONA SHERWOOD
San Miguel Street
9.5" x 14" (24 cm x 36 cm)
Arches 140 lb. cold press
Watercolor with gouache

The textures found in *San Miguel Street* help to provide an aged appearance to the buildings and convey the sense of the road being rough and unplanned. Pieces of rice paper were collaged onto the watercolor paper to create the figure in the doorway and give vitality to the areas of pure watercolor that seemed otherwise flat. The combination of painted textures and collage helped enrich the painting.

CARMEN NEWMAN BAMMERT
Eye of the Storm
20" x 30" (51 cm x 76 cm)
Crescent heavyweight illustration board
Watercolor with acrylic, gel, and acrylic
medium

Working in texture allows me the freedom to be creative. Golden heavy-body gel was used to form the circle, inner rectangle, and ridges while organic shapes were done with a palette knife, a comb-like tool, and my fingers. Fluid acrylics were glazed over the dried gel, allowing color to flow into valleys and rest on raised areas, giving the painting an illusion of depth. Pieces of dried paint and acrylic gel were collaged in the center of the circle and other areas. Texture gives this work the needed energy to convey its title, *Eye of the Storm*.

JACK B. BEVIER
Almond Tree Ranch
13" x 24.5" (33 cm x 62 cm)
Crescent 100% rag hot press board
Watercolor with gouache

I am particularly interested in textures found outside: tree bark, stones, grasses, and sky, and I depicted them with meticulous detail in initial drawings. *Almond Tree Ranch* was painted, glazing from light to dark, with a combination of transparent watercolor and white gouache. A dry surface was maintained throughout, with as little water on the brush as possible.

M. C. KANOUSE
Great Egrets
21" x 14" (53 cm x 36 cm)
Lanaquarelle 300 lb. cold press

Texture helps define the feathers, the foliage, and the reflection of the birds on the water in *Great Egrets*. I like to use a light subject against a dark background, with middle values kept to a minimum. A resist applied to the birds was followed by multiple washes. The reflection of the birds was created by gently removing part of the washes in the pattern of the reflection.

FRED MAC NEILL
Northern Village
14" x 20" (36 cm x 51 cm)
Arches 300 lb. cold press
Watercolor with gouache

When I saw this scene in Vermont, I knew the elements and spirit of a painting were present. Some watercolor was used for its transparency, but I primarily used gouache for the opaque effect it provides. Gouache, which will not be disturbed when a wash is used over it, was used for small details and for overpainting colors to add to the texture. The rough grasses and bushes were drybrushed, which was effective with the paper used.

PAULINE EATON
Luna Layers
40" x 30" (102 cm x 76 cm)
Crescent 110 lb. 100% rag illustration board
Watercolor with gouache, Chinese white, and metallic silver

Luna Layers develops design through the parallel elements of cloud formations, made billowy and ephemeral by flooding watery washes against pigment in varying stages of drying. The rolling hills of the background are defined by spattered silver gouache and white paint, while the stark hardness of moonlit cliffs was created by dripping and flinging pigment onto a dry surface. Overall, a wet-edged moon shines with contrasting light provided by spare application of color mixed with metallic silver.

BEVERLY PERDUE NIDA
First Light
24" x 32" (61 cm x 81 cm)
Arches 140 lb. cold press
Watercolor with gouache

Texture was very critical in *First Light* since I wanted to set a specific mood and capture the first break of dawn as it illuminated the ocean horizon. To create hard and soft edges, it was important to have just the right amount of moist surface on the paper where the change of lighting occurred. Since two-thirds of the painting is the ocean, I wanted to create interesting subtle changes there. Using bristle slant brushes vigorously, I was able to manipulate the paint, creating texture, drama, and unexpected effects.

MARY WILBANKS
Apparition
22" x 15" (56 cm x 38 cm)
Strathmore Aquarius 140 lb.
Watercolor with acrylic and watercolor
pencils

Texture is an important element
of my acrylic collage paintings.
Following a process similar to
erosion, I paint, print, pour, scratch,
and collage, then I sand and tear
away to allow order to emerge from
the chaos of texture. The shapes
and forms that emerge are more
varied and interesting than anything
I am able to paint. *Apparition* was
inspired by the rock formations at
Montserrat, Spain.

VIRGINIA L. GOULD
Harvest Bowl
14" x 21" (36 cm x 53 cm)
1059 Morilla board
Watercolor with gesso and
transparent ink

The texture in *Harvest Bowl* was created using a number of techniques. After a light watercolor wash was applied, shapes for the fruit and bowl were painted with gesso, with dry colored ink applied and pieces of plastic wrap laid over each fruit. Crumpled wax paper was pressed on top of the bowl after the ink was poured. When dry, all wraps were removed. A gentle sanding with extra-fine sandpaper produced the mottled effect in the background.

BEV REILEY
Jacks and Cat's Eyes
17" x 9" (43 cm x 23 cm)
Winsor and Newton 260 lb. cold press
Watercolor with gesso and gouache

Paintings that communicate texture make us want to touch them to experience the tactile sensations they evoke. *Jacks and Cat's Eyes* presented a challenging exercise in painting contrasting textures. The slick, transparent surface of the marbles and the smooth, red, rubber ball were contrasted with the cracked, pebbled surface of the sidewalk. The jacks are colorful, hard shapes with paint peeling off the edges from hours of play.

JUNE BERRY
Picking Greens
20.5" x 23" (52 cm x 58 cm)
260 lb. paper

The creative process is set in motion by an instinctive response to subject matter that has a richness of detail, pattern, and texture. I prefer to work within a closed composition with a tight underlying geometry, to support a textured surface pattern. Pure watercolor allowed me to build up a dense texture through layers of underpainting without losing the brilliance of the color. A variety of textures in the sky, buildings, trees, and vegetables was depicted using different types of brushstrokes.

MONROE LEUNG
Park Palms
18" x 24" (46 cm x 61 cm)
Arches 140 lb. rough

I painted *Park Palms* on location, where I had watched fourth-of-July fireworks the night before. As I sketched the layout, I thought of the exploding rockets and resulting star shapes; how they burst, blossomed, and drifted down to earth, their lacy trails resembling graceful palm fronds. This fiery display was the motivation of the painting. It was painted wet-in-wet, using a sponge for most of the painting.

LAUREL LAKE McGUIRE
Seaworthy: Gifts of my Father
15" x 19" (38 cm x 48 cm)
Arches 140 lb. cold press

To capture the moment of recognition when the serendipitous union of object, light, and mood catches the eye and mind, it is necessary to portray the essence of each article completely. More useful than any trick or technique is a total concentration on a particular surface. If I am painting concrete, for example, I focus on what concrete feels like, how it takes the light, and what its properties are. This internal dialogue guides the hand and brush, and in painting any subsequent element, I must refocus and reestablish a new internal dialog that expresses the memories and emotions that are evoked.

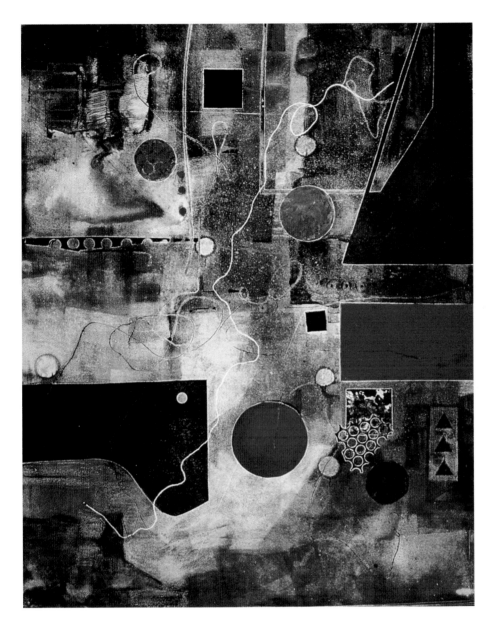

BEA JAE O'BRIEN
The Concert
18" x 15" (46 cm x 38 cm)
Rives BFK heavyweight
Watercolor with watercolor pencil

My desire was to express the atmosphere of a concert, suggesting the orchestra, the drama of color and lighting, and the excitement and anticipation of the event. To achieve the textures, I sprayed a liberally color-rolled plate with water. I then placed cut and paint-rolled papers onto the plate in various patterns. I used an etching press to pull the monotype print, and then used watercolor pencils to enhance the textures.

CHANG FEE-MING
Morning Majesty
22" x 30" (55 cm x 75 cm)
Schut rough surface

I am inspired by my environment, from Malaysia to Bali, and the regional textiles, with their variety of texture and color. In *Morning Majesty*, the opacity of the sarong contrasts with the transparency of the lace kebaya and the conveyed sense of intimacy of the skin beneath. The smooth, glossy skin of the foot contrasts with the grainy texture of the sand. Careful attention to textures helps bring out the physical reality of the young ladies and brings tangibility to the glory of a Balinese morning.

ROBERTA P. LINTNER
Wave Patterns XI
15" x 19.5" (38 cm x 50 cm)
Aquarius II 80 lb.
Watercolor with gesso, gouache, and acrylic

Working on gessoed Aquarius paper, I let the paint flow freely, hoping to capture the mystery of the ocean. I started with watercolor, working wet-in-wet, and then used gouache, randomly spraying the surface with water. Finally, I spattered white acrylic to interpret the feeling of ocean foam. This technique gave a strong feeling of the fluid quality of the ocean.

DONALD W. PATTERSON
Backwater
19" x 26" (48 cm x 66 cm)
Arches 300 lb. cold press
Watercolor with gouache

When I first spot a subject that catches my attention, texture is often the one element above all that appeals to my creative process. In *Backwater*, I found the tangle of reeds an irresistible challenge to paint. To capture the essence of the reeds' texture, I used masking fluid to draw the reeds, and painted the negative areas first. I then removed the masking and painted the positive areas.

NAOMI COX
Stargate
14" x 20" (36 cm x 51 cm)
Arches 140 lb. rough

I see texture as a creative device to pull the viewer into a picture. In an abstract painting, texture becomes even more magical, with the tactile immediacy drawing the viewer into a world that exists nowhere else. My guiding thought as I worked on *Stargate* was to create a world of distance. When I added abstract texture to the receding planes using sprinkled salt and crumbled plastic wrap, it was done to draw the viewer along with me into those distant planes.

ANNA CHEN
Prelude to a Still Moment
25" x 40" (64 cm x 102 cm)
Arches 140 lb. hot press

I was amazed by the intricate curved lines that formed interesting geometric patterns on the surfaces of glass Christmas-tree balls. Under strong light, they created sensational reflections and shadows. In replicating these effects in *Prelude to a Still Moment*, cool blue colors dominate the whole painting to give the effect of calm and still moments. Textures were created working wet-in-wet with plenty of water, starting from a small area, then extending to larger areas. After glazing light to dark and allowing to dry, more values were added to create dramatic effects that complete the painting.

CATHERINE ANDERSON
Hakuna Mootata
22" x 30" (56 cm x 76 cm)
Lanaquarelle 300 lb. hot press

In each of my paintings my goal is to convey a feeling of aliveness, peace, and my love of life. *Hakuna Mootata* has over one-hundred layers of paint to achieve a foggy glow, depth, and texture that creates life. The cows were masked through the entire layering process and worked on at the end. Each wash was applied with a 4 3/4-inch Hake brush on 300 lb. hot press paper. Textures on the cows and grasses were created with the masking fluid. The roughness of the grass, the muddy cows, and the softness of the fog combined to make a satisfying composition.

JOSEPH BOHLER
Ana Maria–La Candelera
28.5" x 36.5" (72 cm x 93 cm)
Arches 444 lb. cold press

I found Ana Maria in a small Mexican village making beeswax candles for her church, the last of her generation to enact this old process. Texture is unifying effect that holds this piece together because it helps create the essence of times past. Soft and textured areas in the painting produce contrast and interest. I primarily used drybrush to give an old-time feeling to the building and surroundings.

WOLODIMIRA VERA WASICZKO
Deep Blue Moment
20" x 30" (51 cm x 76 cm)
Crescent 100% rag hot press
Watercolor with acrylic and gesso

A floral subject, such as *Deep Blue Moment*, lends itself beautifully to texture. After a light coat of gesso, the dried surface was flooded with pale washes of watercolor. I then began the layering process, allowing drying time in between. Instant texturing was produced on fairly wet paint by spattering water in certain areas and spraying alcohol in others. A toothbrush, sponges, and rubber nibs were used to scrape and drag the paint, as well as to wipe out areas, creating diverse effects and resulting in a work with a non-static approach to a realistic subject.

MARY ANN BECKWITH
Origins Secret I
44" x 30" (112 cm x 76 cm)
Arches 140 lb. hot press
Watercolor with ink and watercolor
pencil

The image of *Origins Secret I* was
developed by painting multiple layers of texture. Fiber cobwebs were
tautly stretched over the paper and
completely saturated with clear
water until they adhered to the
surface. The area was then painted
with washes of lightfast inks and
watercolor, and once dry, the fiber
was removed, leaving its imprint.
Templates were laid over the
surface, and diluted white watercolor was sprayed unevenly, leaving
an additional layer of spattered
paint. The final development of the
painting included washes, lifting,
and enhancement with watercolor
pencils.

LINDA L. SPIES
Lewis and Clark
20.5" x 26.5" (52 cm x 67 cm)
Strathmore 500 lb. hot press bristol
Watercolor with watercolor pencil

Moored in shallow, sun-dappled water on the bank of the Missouri River, this pair of weathered wooden boats caught my eye. I floated colors on the board areas, tilted the paper to let them run, and spattered more colors over the surface to capture the mottled reflection on the rough, wooden texture of the red boat. Color was pulled off along the top of the gunwales and the side of the boat with a chisel-cut brush handle, separating light from shadows. The diagonal of the white rope draws the viewer into the surfaces of the boats.

MADELEINE BURKE-FANNING
Tribal Affairs
22" x 30" (56 cm x 76 cm)
Lanaquarelle 140 lb. cold press
Watercolor with ink

By allowing the line and texture to
show through my subject, the
Indians were made part of the land
around them, besides adding a
spiritual and mystical quality. The
soft, feathery texture was created
by pouring indigo blue and ink on
wet paper. A strong spray of water
moved the ink around and created
puddles. After drying, I wet the
painting again and poured thinned,
white ink and covered it with plastic
wrap, which I pulled to create line
and direction. I let the painting dry
again, and used white pastel pencil
to draw the figures over the dark
ink. The work was completed by
applying watercolor in both positive
and negative.

ALLAN HILL
Central Steppes
22.5" x 30" (57 cm x 76 cm)
Arches 140 lb. hot press
Watercolor with acrylic

The chaos and chance associated with out-of-control flowing paint and the resulting texture and forms were central in deciding the composition of my painting. I prefer to imply nature's imagery rather than illustrate natural forms. The fluid qualities of watermedia on smooth paper fit my spontaneous approach. Techniques used in *Central Steppes* included pouring and spreading pigment, spare brushwork, and adding pieces of paper, cloth, and glass to achieve textures and edges. These prepared papers were then torn for collaging. Texture's unexpected and ambiguous qualities defined the forms and movements that pulled the work together.

EMILY JAMES
The Hearth
15" x 20" (38 cm x 51 cm)
Watercolor board

The Hearth was inspired by the home of *Gone with the Wind* author Margaret Mitchell, a once stately mansion that has fallen into disrepair. Balancing the suggestion of the linear structure of the room, the feel of aged, water-damaged, textured surfaces, and a subtle amount of warmth of memories provided the challenge. Exciting textures were created by applying Liquitex Gelex with a brush and palette knife to areas before painting. The Gelex doesn't totally resist the watercolor, resulting in a visual effect of cracked plaster and charred logs in the fireplace.

MARY JANE BELL
Reflections
15" x 22" (38 cm x 56 cm)
Arches 140 lb. medium

The essence of *Reflections* is the contrast of the hard-surface textures of the paperweights to the designs within them. Depicting the hardness of glass and metal using pure watercolor provided a challenge. In the background, I worked wet-in-wet to create the soft texture. Dry wash was used on the paperweights, gradually building up from light to dark. I tried to save the whites, but in several areas I used a razor blade to retrieve highlights.

MARY ELLEN ANDREN
Remembrance
20" x 23" (51 cm x 58 cm)
Crescent 114 cold press board
Watercolor with acrylic and collage

For *Remembrance*, a ground layer was established and a somber mood was set. Calligraphy was used between layers of transparent color and torn papers built up the collage, helping create texture and dynamics. Texture was extremely important in conveying the fragmentation of lives in this personal and deeply felt memorial to Flight 800.

JANE OLIVER
The Store
16" x 20" (41 cm x 51 cm)
90 lb. hot press
Watercolor with acrylic

Working on dry paper, I first applied frisket in flat patterns and painted with thin acrylics. After removing the frisket, I soaked the paper, crumpled it in a ball, rolled it out flat, and while still wet, applied washes of watercolor. I appreciate this technique for the way water-color falls on the crumpled paper and the brighter colors resulting from the acrylic underpainting.

L. HERB RATHER, JR.
Glass and Brass
30" x 22" (76 cm x 56 cm)
Arches 140 lb. rough

I chose the subject primarily for
the intricate textures portrayed.
Keeping patterning as the central
focus, the cut-glass vase provided
the opportunity to depict deep-cut
patterns and shallow frosted-cut
areas emphasized by the refracted
light patterns. The hammered-brass
bowl and crocheted tablecloth
offered contrasting textures particularly suited to the transparent glazes
of the watercolors. My primary
technique was direct painting on
dry paper; some edges were softened with tissue while still wet.

PATSY SMITH
Winds of Autumn
40" x 60" (102 cm x 152 cm)
100% rag 6-ply museum board
Watercolor with acrylic

Watercolor pigment was poured, dripped, and dappled to produce a mottled surface on the board. Once dry, thinned acrylic was glazed over, scraped through, and painted in linear strokes to tie the shapes together. Larger shapes were built to add stability to all the textures and smaller shapes. The feeling of wind through the leaves was enhanced by a final glazing of deep-colored darks.

JOHN A. NEFF
Appreciating Homer
20" x 28" (51 cm x 71 cm)
tissue on double weight
illustration board
Watercolor and acrylic

Acrylic washes were randomly used to create a surface texture. When pleased with the initial washes and shapes, I reviewed my collection of prints and slides from an exhibition of Winslow Homer's work for placement in the composition. I drew outlines of the figures on a separate sheet and cut them out for arrangement in the background. Controlled brushwork was used for the final painting.

HELLA BAILIN
Roosters
29" x 21" (74 cm x 53 cm)
Whatman illustration board rough
Watercolor with acrylic and casein

Starting with a charcoal drawing, I painted the background with transparent watercolor in ochres, reds, and sepia. Torn pieces of magazine and newspaper were pasted on and glazed over with a thin coat of raw umber acrylic. Lighter parts of the roosters were then wiped away and a sponge was used to create texture. After drying, I applied red casein on the roosters' heads, white casein highlights on their bodies, and accent colors in several areas to complete the painting.

JEAN DEEMER
Intervention
24.5" x 32" (62 cm x 81 cm)
Indian Village 300 lb. rough over
Saunders Waterford 300 lb. rough

My focus on geological formations—something new formed from shattered remnants—translated well using 300 lb. rough papers to capture the inherent texture of nature. The work began intuitively, glazing washes of color, scumbling, blotting, adding lines or marks, and artificially aging the paper to convey the essence of time. The paper was cut and peeled back to create layers. The Indian Village paper was torn apart and new shapes were created, with some layering and additional color glazes. Scraps from my collage bin were used for the intervention.

DONNA WATSON
Asian Harmony
20" x 26" (51 cm x 66 cm)
Crescent watercolor board hot press
Watercolor with watercolor crayons,
gouache, and collage

Texture adds interest and excitement to my paintings, and my choice of materials is directly related to the types of textures I want to create. Hot-press watercolor board allows for special effects of splattering, scratching, and moving the paint around. I started with watercolors and watercolor crayons and then added gouache in layers, allowing parts of the underpainting to show through. Rice papers and handmade papers were added for extra texture, and paint was again layered over parts of the papers to achieve a balance of textured and rest areas.

CAROLANN WATTERSON
Abstract Noir
22" x 30" (56 cm x 76 cm)
Arches 140 lb. hot press
Watercolor and gouache

The composition of abstract forms in this painting is designed using texture only. Created using acetate shapes and crushed dye paper, gouache covers some areas of color to create a veil and subdue the negative spaces.

KATHLEEN PAWLEY
Patio Patterns
22" x 29" (56 cm x 74 cm)
Strathmore 3-ply bristol vellum

The challenge of *Patio Patterns* was to interpret the diamond patterns of the iron table and chair, while retaining the integrity of the wash of the background darks. Bristol vellum, being less absorbent, made it possible to carry the wash through the iron work pattern, and return later with a small bristle brush to scrub out suggestions of the grids. The intense sunlight casting the shadow pattern on the patio maintained the flow of the circular patterns that repeat diagonally across the composition. Dark watercolor splashed onto the flowerpot and geranium add solidity and contrast to the ethereal feeling of light.

MAXINE CUSTER
Ancient Ones
22" x 18" (56 cm x 46 cm)
Arches Aquarius II
Watercolor with acrylic, gouache, and
watercolor crayon

Use of texture suggests ancient facades, creates mood, gives the essence of past civilization, and serves as an invitation to the viewer to linger and explore the content of *Ancient Ones*. In the process of painting, the ancient figures seemed to emerge entirely on their own. This work developed using techniques that included layering of paint, transparent glazes, scratches with various tools, resists, and stamps I carved from a variety of materials.

FRANK MILAUSKAS
Marking Time
22" x 30" (56 cm x 76 cm)
Arches 300 lb. cold press

The success of *Marking Time* depended on total concentration on texture. The lobster markers, originally brightly painted, are now faded and worn, the ropes now salt-eroded, and the post and roughly hewn split-rail fence are deeply weathered. Once, these markers identified prize lobster areas off the coast of Monhegan Island, Maine, now, they are simply marking time with quiet dignity.

PAINTING LIGHT AND SHADOW

There is poetry outdoors; artists can learn about light by observing natural light from early dawn through noonday to the last light of evening. At every moment the light changes, ever so slowly, so subtly we hardly notice. This colored light mixes with the air and touches all objects in our landscape. The beautiful blue sky plays upon upward planes. It runs across our shoulders and through our hair. This same colored light falls on the treetops, on the grass, on the roofs of houses; it glistens on the back of a horse who trots by. This light shines equally on all things and ties our beautiful world together.

Sunlight lights up the world while adding its color to the forms in our landscape. Even the moisture in the air changes the intensities and values of the light and mixes to create its own color. A good painting is touched with this color, one light, seen as it moves through air and space. As the light moves toward us, it intensifies in its brilliance until finally it reaches the closest of the picture planes.

As the light adds its warmth, shadows play upon forms with all their coolness. Shadows remain the same in color throughout a painting, only losing intensity as they recede into the picture plane. The light of the sky always affects those shadows on the upward planes in our landscape.

In the past, shadows were painted as dark and colorless. They were painted then as we now would only paint in north studio light or at the strange and colorful last light of day. The shadows were dramatic in their starkness, making the air and light even warmer and brighter. It was Caravaggio who first lit a candle behind models so we could enter the shadows and move through them. Then came impressionism, and the great painters observed that shadow and light were complements to each other, with one always stronger in intensity than the other. They showed how at noon time, colored light from the sun joins the colored light of the sky and mixes together, beating down upon the earth and sending up a magnificent reflected light. It was Sargent and Sorolla and many others who took this light and added it to local color.

Painters began to leave out the local color when modern painting began. Perhaps if the sky in early morning contained a soft yellow light with pearly gray-blue sky over it, the blues were left out and only the yellows were painted. Or if a cool purple-blue shadow ran across the gray trees, the gray was left out and only the purple-blue was painted. Even such a landscape will appear true to our eyes. Artists work in their own creative way and add much to their painting through their unique understanding and expression of light and shadow.

YOLANDA FREDERIKSE
Bay Watchers
22" x 30" (56 cm x 76 cm)
Arches 300 lb. cold press

Light, the effects of light, and transparency are the subjects of *Bay Watchers*. Intense summer sun penetrates the thin fabric of the beach umbrella and is absorbed by and reflected on the draped towels, the platform surface, and the wet skin of the lifeguards. The brilliant blue background is meant to be intimate yet isolating, portraying the lifeguards as both ordinary and monumental. I used a combination of staining and opaque watercolors, allowing the paper and paint to dry between glazes.

JOAN M. BORYTA
Twilight Hour
22" x 30" (56 cm x 76 cm)
Winsor and Newton 140 lb. cold press

Twilight Hour was painted to catch the interplay of suffusive light cast by the setting sun and the rising moon. While the sun is still high enough to reflect glowing light off the windows, it is also low enough to cast a subtle shadow onto the foreground. I selected a strong, dense color for a one-coat application of the sky and a transparent layering of cool blue shadow in the foreground snow, keeping in mind the importance of luminosity.

WARD P. MANN
Dory
19.5" x 25" (50 cm x 64 cm)
Arches double elephant 240 lb. cold press

Dory was painted in Gloucester, Massachusetts where I found a simple subject that became more interesting through the enhancement of the contrast between bright and muted colors, detail and suggested form, and most importantly, light and dark. Form and cast shadows are essential to the composition's completion and they make a strong statement about the boat and water reflections and surface detail. Transparent watercolor was ideal for recreating the translucent nature of shadows. I painted around the white areas with the darkest dark and then worked dark into the shadow of the dory.

ROBERT SAKSON
Rexall
22" x 30" (56 cm x 76 cm)
Arches 140 lb. cold press rough

One of the last of its kind, this old drugstore in Hopewell, New Jersey caught my attention. The shadow areas were done using a mixture of Van Dyck brown, ultramarine blue, and Winsor violet mixed with aquapasto medium to retain life. The shadows strengthen the whites and hold them together. Colors were applied directly on the paper to keep the image fresh.

JEAN KALIN
Caribbean Series: Cayman Eagle
18" x 18" (46 cm x 46 cm)
Arches 140 lb. cold press

On Grand Cayman Island, the hot sun brings out texture and contrast—sheen on skin, flat black braids, bleached concrete, and strong shadows. Since I enjoy painting light and people, I was drawn to this woman with her tattoo and casual posture. Working from color notes and photographs I started painting wet-in-wet, pushing the colors, and applying many layers, letting each dry completely, using less and less water as I continued. I finished with drybrush for details and to sharpen the textured effects.

MARGARET EBBINGHAUS BURCH
Honey and Orange Marmalade
22" x 30" (56 cm x 76 cm)
Arches 300 lb. cold press

I arranged the objects in *Honey and Orange Marmalade* into a vignette style with a sheet of glass positioned behind them to reflect the light and achieve a high-keyed look. The work was unified using techniques such as wet-in-wet, transparent layers, working from light to dark, and large areas to small. I emphasized the texture in the many types of glass vessels used—transparent, reflective, and flat, dull pieces. Cast shadows added a sense of dramatic light and natural light added a sense of nostalgic warmth.

FREDRICK T. KUBITZ
South Wharf–Padanaram, New Bedford, MA c. 1920
22" x 30" (56 cm x 76 cm)
Arches 300 lb. cold press

The inspiration for this painting came from an old black-and-white photograph showing the serenity of summer bathed in direct sunlight. Warmth in the light-sand beach was repeated in the buildings, dock, distant background, and lazy summer clouds, and was complemented by darker blue water and sky. Horizontal bands of warm and cool colors were purposely alternated to enhance the feeling of light. The white accents reinforcing the presence of direct sunlight were masked prior to starting the first washes. Darker values were introduced with the beach grass, buildings, and large schooner.

DARYL BRYANT
Cows at Church
15" x 22" (38 cm x 56 cm)
Winsor and Newton 140 lb. cold press

Living in southern California has had a big influence upon my choice of color, location, and subject. The play of light upon objects and the colors in shadows have long fascinated me. Using a palette of mostly transparent colors, I began painting washes with plenty of water and culminated with heavier applications of pure color applied directly to the paper. Located in a charming small town, the church is where my sister was married and provides me with the emotional connection to my subject that I find an important element in my work.

MARGARET R. MANRING
Joanna in Dress-Up
14" x 20.5" (36 cm x 52 cm)
Arches 140 lb. cold press

I am always looking for light, its reflection, absorption, movement, and how it transforms the objects in its path. To portray light, I make use of the transparency of watercolor, the characteristics of the paper, and the simple techniques of direct painting—wet-in-wet, scrubbing, and some drybrush. I pay close attention to details like highlights. There are no highlights in the eyes due to the diffused light beneath the hat brim; and in the more direct light, the lip highlight is soft. Most defined is the bead highlight, because it lies in the strongest light. Black feathers and some areas of velvet serve as foils for the light-reflective portions of the painting.

PAT BERGER
Is Yesterday, Today, Tomorrow?
22" x 30" (56 cm x 76 cm)
Arches 300 lb. cold press

To create the desired mood, I used multiple layers of blue-gray and brownish washes, overlaying the glazes. The painting depicts past violence that continues into the present and, perhaps, the future. Mystery was created by keeping the figures in shadow with the ground providing the only light and the prone figure having the only definition. Use of shadow interconnects images of the past and present.

VIRGINIA ABBATE THOMPSON
The Fourth Chair
22" x 30" (56 cm x 76 cm)
Lanaquarelle 140 lb.
Watercolor with gouache and colored pencil

Many of my paintings use light and shadow and suggest something beyond what is shown. My three sons used these chairs when they were little. In this painting, "the fourth chair" represents the fourth child I wanted, but never had. Sunlight coming through the kitchen door leaves a shadow of the unseen chair. Using primarily transparent watercolor, I airbrushed the floor and walls and used splatters of gouache to indicate points of light and reflection and colored pencil for other detail.

LAEL NELSON
100% Cotton
39" x 27" (100 cm x 69 cm)
Arches 300 lb. cold press
Watercolor with gouache

Once the initial drawing was completed, values were painted in burnt umber, dark areas were applied in a thick paste form, the middle values were washed in, and the white areas were simply left unpainted. A dark underpainting makes the colors richer and more intense with monochromatic colors enhancing the work's strong statement. High contrast creates the light and brings the figure bathed in sunshine to life.

GEORGE E. KOUNTOUPIS
Granada, Spain
22" x 30" (56 cm x 76 cm)
Arches 300 lb.
Watercolor with acrylic

The brightly lit areas in this work are produced by surrounding the pure white of the paper with darks. Middle values relating to the light were made slightly lighter and warmer. The subject was side-lit, allowing me to place the strong lights on the buildings facing the sun. The strongest darks were then carefully placed next to these sunlit areas. In proportioning this work, I allotted approximately three-fourths of the painting for shadow and one-fourth for light.

GEORGE E. KOUNTOUPIS
Flower Market—Portugal
22" x 30" (56 cm x 76 cm)
Arches 300 lb.

By placing the painting three-fourths in shadow of a middle value as shown, I used darks and lights to emphasize the figure and flowers, with the lightest value against the figure and the darkest value being the figure itself. Colorful flowers are dramatized by maintaining shadows with grayer and cooler tones. The arrangement of the shadows frames the subject and gives a sense of light direction.

ANTHONY VENTURA
Edge of the Woods
10" x 14" (25 cm x 37 cm)
Arches 140 lb. cold press

The beautiful play of light coming through the trees, emphasizing the sycamores, first caught my eye. With this image in mind, I kept the colors warm and vibrant, working wet-in-wet on dry paper, shaping the sycamores as the work progressed. Shadows were painted with reflected light, then the darker trees and shadows were added to strengthen the light tones and add balance. Light was achieved by carefully using the white of the paper, warm colors, and dark accents.

JORGE BOWENFORBÉS
Reading Shakespeare
22" x 30" (56 cm x 76 cm)
Arches 140 lb. cold press

I created a visual interpretation of depth by painting the entire foreground in shadow. This is important when working with an almost monochromatic palette, where the darks are used to establish form and animate the trees. Gradating shadows established convincing contrasts throughout the painting, with glazing serving as the predominate technique.

PRISCILLA E. KREJCI
Under the Eaves
11" x 30" (28 cm x 76 cm)
Lanaquarelle 300 lb. cold press

This painting was inspired by birds I found huddled under the eaves during a cool, rainy day in Lucerne, Switzerland. The muted daylight provided faint shadows that I was able to recreate by letting the paint and water interact with a little directional guidance from me.

JOANNA MERSEREAU
Noon at Mission La Purisima
14" x 30" (36 cm x 76 cm)
Lanaquarelle 300 lb. cold press

The theme of *Noon at Mission La Purisima* was the concept of brilliant, blinding, noonday light as seen at a California mission. This subject was chosen as one of a series of paintings illustrating my book, *Dark Mission*. Transparent watercolor was used, with complementary colors providing outlines and creating an aura around the various elements.

JEAN COLE
Iris #3
30" x 45" (76 cm x 114 cm)
Arches 140 lb. cold press

Before photographing a subject, I look for dramatic lighting, high contrast, and good shadow forms that help describe it. I take pictures only on sunny days, not minding if some colors burn out because the shadows then take on a lot of color. Transparent watercolor works best to capture the luminosity of color in floral subjects and I use layered glazes to build up color for depth and intensity. I combine several colors in one area, first painting the local color then going over with a shadow color, trying to find as much color as possible in the shadows.

MARGO BARTEL
Majestic Sentinel
22" x 30" (56 cm x 76 cm)
Arches 140 lb. cold press
Watercolor with acrylic

I do not approach my painting with a preconceived subject in mind. Instead, I find my subject by working with thin glazes of color over color, playing dark against light with shape and color variations, and using differing brush-strokes. While trying to stay as abstract as possible, I am always excited when the subject begins to take form.

JACK R. BROUWER
Afternoon Rain
14" x 21" (36 cm x 53 cm)
Arches 140 lb. cold press

As a beginning painter, I would draw a light bulb on the border of my paintings to remind me of the constant importance of light. Now, I watch for unexpected light that can create drama and excitement in my painting. It was the sudden emergence of the sun after a rainstorm that produced such an effect in *Afternoon Rain.* I paint in transparent watercolor letting the white of the paper carry the strongest whites and add contrast with strong deeper colors that maximize excitement and interest.

ROBERT E. HEYER
Prairie Wagon
22" x 30" (56 cm x 76 cm)
Arches 140 lb. rough

I find interesting shapes and textures in subject matter that is in some stage of deterioration. Shadows in my paintings express mood, act as a transitional element between shapes, and describe a surface attribute such as rough, weathered wood and rusted iron wheels. Keeping the white of the paper as my white, I use a rough paper to produce the needed texture along with transparent watercolors.

MONROE LEUNG
Summer in Soweto
20" x 25" (51 cm x 64 cm)
Arches 140 lb. rough

Summer in Soweto was made from on-location sketches and photos. The subject presented ideal conditions for sunlight and shadows; the corrugated roof and balcony cast deep shadows that contrasted sharply with the sunlit areas. Shadows gave depth and vibrancy to the painting and most of the paint was applied directly on a dry surface or over dry color.

NAT LEWIS
Salt Water Farm
16.5" x 23.5" (42 cm x 60 cm)
Arches 300 lb. hot press

Fascinated by old white houses, it is the dramatic patterns of light and dark, rather than the houses themselves, that inspire me. While most house paintings depict shadows cast on sunny surfaces, I have chosen an opposite approach, capturing fleeting moments when the sun moves from one side of the house to the other, leaving narrow shafts of light within the shadow. I began by covering the entire surface with a pale yellow wash and masking the sun glints before painting the shadow color, keeping the wash clean and uninterrupted. Sunny patterns are then exposed when the masking is removed.

ALLISON CHRISTIE
Bamboo VIII
19" x 14" (48 cm x 36 cm)
Arches 300 lb. cold press

My main focus is on the designs created by cast shadows and the forward movement these patterns provide for a realist's subject. After sketching in the dominant foreground and midground lines, I determined where the shadows should lay and painted them first. Using burnt sienna and French ultramarine as my base, a wide range of soft warms to soft cools to ink black was achieved. Surrounding color influences were added for interest and contrast and the shadows helped heighten the contrast of the older, drier leaves with the younger, supple, green leaves.

RANULPH BYE
Bedminster Landscape
15" x 21" (38 cm x 53 cm)
Arches 140 lb. cold press

Painted on an overcast day without strong light or shadows, *Bedminster Landscape* depicts strong value contrasts of woods and fields against white snow. The snow areas are untouched paper with slight variations where the snow has melted. Drybrush was used in some areas to indicate grassy texture. With the absence of sunlight, values were simplified and darker than those found on a clear day. Spontaneity was the key in this work, with every area painted directly and very little going over later.

RICHARD J. SULEA
Barn with Yard
14" x 21" (36 cm x 53 cm)
Arches 300 lb. cold press
Watercolor with gouache

The use of light to define form is of utmost importance in my work. In painting architectural forms in sunlight, careful attention to value is achieved by successive light washes that are allowed to dry before the next one is applied. Three to ten washes may be applied to any given form to achieve the correct value relationships in the composition.

S. OHRVEL CARLSON
Annisquam Fair
17" x 23" (43 cm x 58 cm)
140 lb. cold press

The backlighting on the figures and objects required a different pattern of sunlight and shadow than would occur if the light came from the left or right. Beyond that, I used a traditional English technique of building up layers of transparent color from light to dark and transparent to opaque.

ROBERT S. OLIVER
Chinese Junk
14" x 20" (36 cm x 51 cm)
Arches 140 lb. rough

Chinese Junk was painted in my studio from annotated sketches done on location. The atmosphere of the setting was clear and crisp and called for a strong value change throughout the painting. Using wet-in-wet and drybrush techniques, I utilized the rough surface of the paper to reflect the darks and lights while softening the edges.

HENRY W. DIXON
Arches
34.5" x 20.5" (88 cm x 52 cm)
Arches 140 lb.

Blending light and shadow to
provide the basis of a pleasing
composition, I paint on dry
paper, which allows me to use
the white of the paper for areas
of lightest light. Using the light
with varying shadow values lets
me bring out the main artistic
qualities of the work's subject,
the arches.

GLORIA PATERSON
Cibola
31" x 40" (79 cm x 102 cm)
Museum board
Watercolor with acrylic, markers,
and crayon

The title *Cibola* is taken from the Spanish conquistadors who pursued the seven cities of Cibola, where the streets were reportedly paved with gold. Initial studies of the painting were cut, torn, and applied as collage elements to achieve a flat dimension, interesting surface, and straight edges. These areas were then painted over, some by using brayers. Dark, medium, and light grays and blacks were used to create movement throughout the painting.

JACK DENNEY
Church Ruins—Mykonos
16" x 22" (41 cm x 56 cm)
Arches 300 lb. cold press

Shadows enhance composition, mood, storytelling, and light as well as presenting a stage for complementary color value. The repeated shapes of the major walls and the dominant backlit sky in *Church Ruins—Mykonos* required imaginative use of a full palette. A primary challenge was representing the whitewashed walls using color. The sky and walls were painted wet-in-wet using transparent watercolors.

ANN PEMBER
Peony Birth
14.5" x 21.5" (37 cm x 55 cm)
Waterford 140 lb. cold press

Since a flower is the main subject of this work, I paid particular attention to the way light shines through the petals and over the various forms. Dramatic lighting, coupled with an up-close perspective, conveys an intimate, almost abstract look at flowers. Light creates pattern, reflects colors, and gives life to the subject, and fairly dark backgrounds provide contrast and drama. I paint around whites, pre-wet areas and let colors mix on the paper. When the right intensity is achieved on the first try, the result is fresh and luminous.

GEORGE GIBSON
Manaus Market
21" x 29" (53 cm x 74 cm)
Arches 300 lb.

Looking down over a canvas-covered market and the inclined street beyond it, the changing elevations of the subject were of particular interest to me. Light and shadow, the shapes they create, and the play of sunlight throughout the composition were an irresistible challenge. The combinations of light and shadow were achieved by close attention to values and textures of the subject.

HARRIET ELSON
Mosiac Family
12" x 21" (31 cm x 53 cm)
Arches 300 lb. cold press

Mosaic Family represents the coming together of different pieces to form one entity. The people are painted light and bright with hard edges to strengthen and keep them as one unit. The viewer is brought into the painting with muted light shapes around the group. Light is essential in my paintings to directing and holding the viewer's eye.

GREGORY B. TISDALE
Middletown
17" x 27.5" (43 cm x 69 cm)
Morilla 130 lb.

In *Middletown*, the entire painting is backlit, and shadow serves as the stage of the painting. The painting is done in almost complete shadow with the only direct shadows found on the deck of the ship. The image of the ship on the ice is a reflection, and the streetlights in the foreground fail to cast a shadow as their light is diminished by the coming of the dawn. Other shadows are muted or diffused and are not immediately recognized.

M. C. KANOUSE
Frey's Barn—Morning
17" x 25" (43 cm x 64 cm)
Lanaquarelle 300 lb. cold press

Early-morning sun provides a vivid contrast, giving solid form to the shadowed areas. Strong contrasts between the high values of the sun and the low values of shadow provide drama to the subject's early-morning time frame. The painting was done with many washes from light to dark. Highlights were established in the shadow pattern by partially removing some areas of the dark paint, changing shadow value and providing form.

KEN SCHULZ
Two Pair
9" x 12" (23 cm x 31 cm)
Strathmore rough

I chose illustration board for *Two Pair* because of the transparency and smoother texture this board offered. I pursued the dark, medium, and light values that relate to the picture planes of foreground, middle ground, and background. Depth and distance were further enhanced by painting the sky first with light washes and adding clouds with shadow and light afterwards. Following a foreground wash, darks were added to the middle ground and foreground. Feather detail was created using shadow and light.

GEORGE J. SHEDD
Waiting at Floyd's
22" x 30" (56 cm x 76 cm)
Bainbridge cold press

The awning over the turn-of-the-century market shadows the window and door beneath while sunlight bathes the steps and the figure to create an interesting value pattern of lights and darks. Working in crisp washes in a light-to-dark sequence, I find that transparent watercolor best conveys the quality I try to achieve, such as the rich, dark colors within the shadows.

GEORGE J. SHEDD
Fresh Air
22" x 30" (56 cm x 76 cm)
Strathmore 300 lb. cold press

Old, nostalgic architecture, such as the house in *Fresh Air*, always offers interesting shapes as subjects for painting. The play of light and broken shadow across the house creates a diagonal pattern that is filled with nuances of color. The fluid quality of transparent watercolor painted simply and directly makes the reflected light in the shadows glow.

EDWIN C. SHUTTLEWORTH
Gulls at Port Kent
17.5" x 23.5" (45 cm x 60 cm)
Arches 140 lb. cold press

Never hesitating to use ambiguous light sources in my work, I feel the design should always be paramount. My subject choices relate to the energy and light that symbolize energy. Cast shadows are useful in unifying the composition and in *Gulls at Port Kent*, the shadow shape on the boarding ramp forms part of the *S* configuration of the dominant white shape.

JULE McCLELLAN
2:30 P.M.–Taking a Break
23.5" x 19" (60 cm x 48 cm)
Strathmore illustration board

*Collection of Sugar Camp Coal
Company*

The shadow of the miner
directs the viewer into the dark
shadows within the building.
Gessoed illustration board lets
the watercolor create textures;
Winsor green, alizarin crimson,
and black used in a fluid manner set the stage for the miner
as the center of interest.
Equipment in the building and
the figure in the shadows were
achieved by wiping away the
images, then repainting where
necessary. The miner and
coiled rope were painted in a
controlled method and the
remainder of the painting was
done using a loose, watery
approach.

NEL BYRD
November
22" x 30" (56 cm x 76 cm)
140 lb. cold press

In creating the composition for *November*, shadows were instrumental in the design and layout. Interesting shapes of the shadow patterns provided the opportunity for color change, reflected light, and values ranging from light-to-dark and warm-to-cool. Elements outside the picture plane were suggested with shadows and in doing so, mundane subjects became unique. Using transparent watercolor, the technique of dropping color into wet wash areas gave me a blend of color and soft edges. I painted on dry paper to achieve sharp edges and saved the white of the paper by painting up to and around the shapes without using any masking.

MORRIS J. SHUBIN
Cannery Row
30" x 40" (76 cm x 102 cm)
Strathmore

To create interest, the upper portion of *Cannery Row* was exaggerated and contrasted against the quiet space of the sky. The large facade was painted in warm and cool colors allowing light and heavy washes to flow into wet areas. The process was repeated, and after each wash had dried, a delicate sponging out was used to achieve a luminous effect. Accents of opaque white were applied as highlights and shadows were exaggerated to reflect the surrounding colors.

PAUL W. NIEMIEC, JR.
Seaworthy
21" x 29" (53 cm x 74 cm)
Arches 300 lb. cold press

In *Seaworthy*, I depicted the soft, diffused light of a calm island morning by working with a limited palette of grays painted in closely related values. Layers of transparent washes were built up to achieve the luminosity and atmospheric haze over the scene. The contrast of light and shadow, the incidences of reflected light, and the balance of warm and cool colors were established by using transparent primary colors in sequential glazes. Shadows were developed with washes of cool, complementary violet tones painted over warm, sand-colored accents.

JOHN McIVER
Ceremony 57
29" x 21" (74 cm x 53 cm)
Waterford 140 lb. cold press
Watercolor with acrylic

My main concern in *Ceremony 57* was the suggestion of groups of figures that would result in an abstract overall pattern. Shadow was used in washes of translucent and transparent paint to establish areas of high and low emphasis. I used a layering of washes, including white, to build texture. Shadow was important to achieve a simplified pattern.

DOROTHY W. BERTINE
Colima Flower Gatherers
22" x 30" (56 cm x 76 cm)
Arches 140 lb. cold press

Shadows play an important role in the creation of interesting positive and negative shapes within a composition. They define forms with irregular edges and textural richness, and increase the luminosity of colors. Furthermore, shadows define the direction of the light, time of day, and weather conditions. I find a painting that is at least 75% shadow much more exciting than a painting representing full light.

DANIEL J. MARSULA
Sanctuary
26" x 26.75" (66 cm x 68 cm)
Arches 140 lb. cold press

In *Sanctuary*, the total feel and emotion of the piece relies on shadows to carry the viewer through the composition. The organic shapes and colors found in nature are my subject of preference. Nature, with its endless supply of shapes and shadows, is best expressed through watercolor and the many techniques available. I've used a combination of drybrush, wet-in-wet, and repeatedly glazed-over transparent washes to create the desired effect.

BARBARA NECHIS
Lunar Series: Moon in Scorpio
22" x 30" (56 cm x 76 cm)
Arches 140 lb. cold press

Without plan or direction, I began this painting by experimenting with shapes. Moonlight came to mind as I added layers of transparent washes that pulled together my numerous initial shapes. Preferring the mood created by close value chords, I used repeated washes to subdue contrasts and excessive light and found that this technique gave the remaining lights a lunar quality. Although negative painting is essential in defining light, I added pattern to the large rock shape at the upper left to prevent a void.

DORLA DEAN SLIDER
Waiting Tables
18.75" x 26.25" (48 cm x 67 cm)
Arches 300 lb.
Watercolor with acrylic and watercolor pencil

The stark, almost black-and-white pattern of the tables and chairs against the sharp shadow created by the high noon sun inspired me to paint *Waiting Tables*. I gessoed the paper as my base to create the texture of the wrought iron. Using a liquid mask on the background tables and chairs, I applied a medium dark wash across the shadow area. I then masked the foreground shadow chair and applied a darker wash, balancing warm and cool and adding the lights last. Touches of watercolor pencils added finishing accents.

DORLA DEAN SLIDER
Sheridan Street
17.5" x 25.5" (44 cm x 65 cm)
Illustration board

The visual power of the water tower over the stark buildings was the inspiration for *Sheridan Street*. The tower and rooftops were masked with a tape that doesn't mar the paper's surface. After first trying a lighter sky wash, I used a darker wash in large vertical strokes to make the sky more dramatic. I played up the rock forms and melted snow on the ground to balance the white areas. Rag illustration board was chosen for its smooth surface that lifts easily, allowing me to work faster and create my own textures.

DONALD W. PATTERSON
Two of a Kind
17" x 26" (43 cm x 66 cm)
Arches 300 lb. cold press
Watercolor with gouache

An integral part of my compositions, shadows are often what draw my attention to a subject. I prefer to paint subjects bathed in late afternoon sun, when the shadows are most exciting. The play of shadows falling on the barn and across the foreground in *Two of a Kind* brings visual appeal to the work. I painted thin washes of opaque white and blue gouache over transparent watercolor to arrive at the precise color and value desired.

JUDY MORRIS
Aunt Edna's Roseville Vase
21" x 29" (53 cm x 74 cm)
Arches 300 lb. cold press
Watercolor with ink

Flowers on my dining-room table are often subjects for my watercolors because I love to paint the vases I collect, and the early-morning light of January creates breathtaking shadows. The background reads as one dark area even though an invented pattern painted in the same value of other colors actually makes up the background shape. This contrasts sharply against the white tablecloth where I've implied lace by painting only a few of shadows. By painting the chair on the right in almost total shadow, I've emphasized the importance of the shadow pattern on the other chair.

JOYCE WILLIAMS
Whirlpool
22" x 30" (56 cm x 76 cm)
Arches 300 lb. cold press
Watercolor with acrylic

Shadows are very much a part of the composition in *Whirlpool*, with the shadow of the haul line being particularly important. The subject, an older lobsterman, was chosen because of his interesting perspective. I used a limited palette of blues and yellows and painted primarily with transparent watercolor and used some acrylic to achieve the texture of the sandy area of the water.

ROBERT T. MILLER
The Cloud Piercer
20" x 31" (51 cm x 79 cm)
Strathmore 114 cold press
Watercolor with acrylic

This subject, located in New Zealand, includes a full range of tonal values. The snow-covered areas of the mountains are contrasted with the deep shadow areas. The cool darks are complemented by the closer mountains painted in warm colors. This very dramatic scene has been captured by carefully contrasting the shadowed areas with the lighted areas.

DOLORES V. PRESTON
Coming Home
19" x 22" (48 cm x 56 cm)
Arches 140 lb. cold press

Winter can be cold, drab, and daunting, but when the sun shines on newly fallen snow, beautiful rainbows appear in the shadows. The transparency of watercolor gives color and sparkle to the shadows. *Coming Home* is made up primarily of these shadows, which enabled me to use color in a winter painting.

ANGELA BRADBURN
Light Play
21.5" x 29.5" (55 cm x 75 cm)
Arches 140 lb. hot press

Light Play is one in a series of paintings from a close, larger-than-life perspective that depends on light and shadow. The subject was chosen because of the impact created by the strong contrast of lights and darks and my goal was to have as much variety as possible while maintaining unity. Since the shadow areas were so dark, I was able to use rich color in the light areas and hold the light-struck look. Contrasting relationships such as light and dark, cool and warm, transparent and opaque, hard edge and soft edge, and representational and abstract were used to achieve variety.

ANGELA BRADBURN
A Closer Look
21.5" x 29.5" (55 cm x 75 cm)
Arches 140 lb. hot press

The subject of *A Closer Look* was chosen because of the strong contrast of lights and darks. Transparent watercolor proved perfect for describing the fragile petals in bright light and charging the shadows with rich, saturated, wet pigment. I painted around the light and used lifting to create a subtle quality and unique color. I used a variety of edges, from crisp to soft to blurred. Shadows define the shapes and contours of the petals and leaves, but also create abstract shapes that dance across the paper.

DOUGLAS WILTRAUT
Family Man
56" x 36" (142 cm x 91 cm)
Arches 114 lb. rough

Family Man is a portrait of my father as he stands in the shadow of the house he built himself. Contrasts were exaggerated in order to bring out sunlight; this was achieved by darkening the shadow so the sunlit part of the subject could be filled with color. The English method of watercolor was used for the colors of the skin, creating a pastel effect similar to the softness of older skin. An elongated diagonal shadow was used to define the musculature of the figure.

JOSEPH BOHLER
Rebecca Painting
21.5" x 29.5" (55 cm x 75 cm)
Arches 300 lb. cold press

The essence of this painting is the natural sunlight falling on my granddaughter Rebecca, casting shadows on the porch. I painted the values around her dark enough to enhance and intensify the light that was reflecting off of her. I used a large 1.5-inch brush for the large shapes in the background and foreground. The figure was painted with a large round brush, glazing several times over the flesh tones to maintain a softness. Spatter was used on the porch and drybrush on the trees and grass.

MICHAEL P. ROCCO
Paesano
21" x 29" (53 cm x 74 cm)
Arches 140 lb. cold press

The shadow in *Paesano* is the unifying and dramatic element of the composition, accentuating the man's face and body. I use strong shadow and light to bring an aspect of dimension, spatial relationship, and the feeling of chiaroscuro to my work. For this painting, I established the major values working around the figure, establishing light and form. I finished by drybrushing texture into the concrete, wood, and flesh.

JUDI BETTS
Leisure Landing
30" x 22" (76 cm x 56 cm)
Arches 140 lb. cold press

I was prompted to paint this picture by the exciting shadows, rich textures, and strong value patterns that made the Adirondack chair appear luminous. In order to convey those visual qualities in my watercolor, I emphasized the shadows around the chair and the linear, dark mid-tone shadows cast by the shingles. I changed the colors as I moved across the page, using gray tones to make the nearby colors more exciting. I varied the shadows in the upper left by using less texture. Deep in the foliage are diagonal light and dark shapes that accent contrasts.

PAT KOCHAN
Bus Stop I
22" x 30" (56 cm x 76 cm)
Arches 140 lb. cold press

The figures in *Bus Stop I* are linked by light and shadow, creating a feeling of solitude that simultaneously shares the existing space. The figures are gradated from light to dark to give them form, and the shadow shapes are kept simple and flat to link the figures and move the viewer's eye across the page. For the shadow areas in the sky, tree, and ground, I layered one glaze of complementary color over another to achieve a rich, deep value of underlying color. For the building, I layered color on color to build each small shape, then covered the large areas with light washes to add depth to the background.

EDWIN L. JOHNSON
Old Fisherman
17" x 27" (43 cm x 69 cm)
Strathmore 100% rag

Usually an artist has only a few moments to capture the viewer's interest. Composition, light, and shadow are paramount to achieving this—with color and detail prolonging the moment. In *Old Fisherman*, the figure is played against the dark of the water with the highlights describing his relaxed attitude. The high backlighting gives the work a sense of drama that makes the painting exciting. Working exclusively in transparent watercolor without any masking materials or opaques, I try to create an interesting arrangement of forms by painting whatever challenges me.

BRAD DIDDAMS
Tight Squeeze II
29.5" x 40" (75 cm x 102 cm)
Arches 555 lb. cold press

Tight Squeeze II is one in a series that studies the effect of light on reflective and semitransparent objects. The coffee pots were chosen to reflect the table and objects on it, and the sugar bowl helps reflect the light source. The set-up was done in a dark room with a single light controlled to fade from one edge of the image to the other. I then photographed the set-up and worked from photographs. While painting, much attention was paid to the highlights to emphasize the structure and add sparkle to the work.

AMANDA JANE HYATT
Melbourne Town Hall
35.5" x 27.5" (90 cm x 70 cm)
Arches 300 g. cold press

With *Melbourne Town Hall*, I created an image of light filtering through the large tree at the right onto the people and reflecting off the building. The subject was chosen for the beauty, solidity, and grandeur of the building compared to the smallness of the people passing by it. Shade under the portico was kept light to show light reflecting off different surfaces. Watercolor easily allows the comparison of light and shadow to be made, the light being the whiteness of the paper or the transparency of the paint. Capturing the light gives a painting magic and a establishes the time frame.

AMANDA JANE HYATT
The High–Oxford, U. K.
35.5" x 27.5" (90 cm x 70 cm)
Arches 300 g. cold press

In *The High–Oxford, U. K.*, I tried to recreate the subtle shade that often dominates an English scene. The details on the buildings were played down and the washes were not fully transparent. An opaqueness, rather than a darkness, was sought to give the impression of a cold, smoky late afternoon. This was achieved by painting the buildings and foreground with up to three washes, then highlighting the dark keyhole shadows with a strong mixture of ultramarine blue, burnt umber, and violet.

GEORGE SOTTUNG
Victoriana
14.5" x 20" (37 cm x 71 cm)
Bainbridge board

I apprenticed under Haddon Sundblom, whose theory was light in all its aspects. His technique was secondary to his awareness of light and shadow and sun-drenched color. In *Victoriana*, I waited for the early afternoon light to warm the colors to the high-keyed palette of the Impressionists. Extraordinary shafts of light break through the picturesque old house and emanate outward. This radiant building, with its high-pitched roof and brilliant windows, is one of the most beautiful along the road.

CORALIE ARMSTRONG
Murray Mouth, South Australia
22" x 29" (56 cm x 74 cm)
Fabriano 600 gsm rough

Light is very important in my painting, both in choice of subject and manner of painting. Colors and tones are affected by light intensity, and the strong Australian sun can drain color. Transparent watercolor allows the light from the paper to show through and is best achieved by a single wash of color. In this painting, the clear distance appealed to me, along with the shapes of the water, hillside, and road. The heavy, rough Fabriano paper provided an interesting texture.

BARBARA GOODSPEED
Sugar House
15" x 22" (38 cm x 56 cm)
Arches 140 lb. cold press

As one of the most essential tools an artist has, light establishes our patterns, values, textures, all the design principles, as well as the mood of the painting. For *Sugar House*, I felt the light source was what would enhance the work and provide a focal point. The sugar house had a good shape, and by changing its color from gray to white, I was able to create spots of light, color, texture, and shadow to compose an interesting painting.

PAT DEWS
Pansies with Grid
21" x 29.5" (53 cm x 75 cm)
Rives BFK
Watercolor with ink and acrylic

This painting is a composite of pansies from numerous photo studies. Flowers are translucent and lend themselves to the subject of light. Using the white of the paper for the dazzling white pansies, I allowed the white to flow from positive to negative spaces without stopping, creating visual contrast and excitement. Small areas of white paper served as areas of light that moved throughout the painting. Good value contrast and strategic darks next to the whites made the whites stand out.

KITTY WAYBRIGHT
Old Shay Drivers
19" x 29" (48 cm x 74 cm)
Arches 300 lb.

A strong light and shadow pattern allows me to see and feel a subject regardless of its actual form. Without light, *Old Shay Drivers* would be flat, and have no life, power, or rhythm. In my drawing, I emphasized shadows, letting their shapes build up form. Similar to working a giant puzzle, I started first with shadows that were done very lightly, and once basic shapes were established, it was push and pull all over the paper, building darks by glazing layers of color.

JANE OLIVER
Autumn Stand
25" x 30" (64 cm x 76 cm)
140 lb. hot press

For landscapes, especially those featuring buildings, I find that shadows help enliven a watercolor. Shadows also give the subject a three-dimensional aspect. In *Autumn Stand*, the jugs of cider, baskets of apples, and pumpkins in the foreground are defined by the light and shadow. I used a wet-in-wet technique and after drying, I glazed transparent layers of color.

DON O'NEILL
Church Along the Canal–Venice
6" x 7.5" (15 cm x 19 cm)
Bockingford 140 lb. cold press
Watercolor and gouache

In *Church Along the Canal—Venice*, I chose a subject that could demonstrate light and shade relationships. Light was all important, so the rich, dark shadow passages were used to accent it. Placing light warm passages adjacent to the cool darks added excitement to the work. The main light area in the painting was established to provide a resting place for the viewer's eye amongst the primary activity that is focused there.

ALICE A. NICHOLS
The Red Chair
28.5" x 21" (72 cm x 53 cm)
Morilla 140 lb.

While traveling in Key West, Florida, I came upon this image of a red chair through an open window. The play of shapes and the contrast of dark against white, the red chair against the green shutters and the white walls was so simple, yet so complex. I applied layers of paint over each area, allowing each to dry, until the strength of contrast I desired was achieved.

HELLA BAILIN
Night Market
28" x 36" (71 cm x 91 cm)
Whatman 90 lb. cold press

Inspired by warm, transparent lights contrasted with the darker, cool shadows, *Night Market* was created from sketches made in Hydra, Greece. Bright colors on the figures and wares were accented against the cool background. The background was painted wet-in-wet, leaving some of the white paper to create highlights. After the paper dried, the figures and detail were applied.

JANET POPPE
Morning Walk
28" x 36" (71 cm x 91 cm)
Fabriano 140 lb. rough

Seeking to capture the morning light of autumn in New York City, I played light and dark shadow forms on the moving people and dogs to create a center of interest. Working with a limited palette, the rough surface paper allowed the paint to settle into the many crevices, which added extra color density and sparkle. The paint was applied wet-in-wet in bold strokes, leaving a good amount of white paper and continually working the entire surface in detail and texture.

NICOLAS P. SCALISE
John in Doorway–Meriden, CT
30" x 16" (76 cm x 41 cm)
Arches 140 lb. cold press

I look for an emotional response in choosing a subject matter. John, the shoemaker, emerges from the darkened doorway and waits with anticipation for customers. Shadow plays a major role in setting the mood and becomes the unique aspect of the painting. My disciplined approach starts with compositional studies, followed with careful drawings, and then a build-up of layers of paint.

DONNA L. WATSON
Oriental Passages
20" x 26" (51 cm x 66 cm)
Crescent hot press
Watercolor with gouache, crayon,
and collage

The Asian theme of *Oriental Passages* brought certain words to mind—harmony, balance, and mystery. With shadow supplying the mystery as well as the balance to my paintings, I try to further balance light or quiet areas and passages with dark shapes and textures. Although I use a number of aqueous media in my work, usually my shadow areas are done with transparent watercolors.

JAMES J. GLEESON
Carnival
25" x 30" (63 cm x 76 cm)
Arches 140 lb. rough

San Francisco has a wonderful light, which becomes clearer and stronger as the year progresses. *Carnival* was painted in October when the light is optimum. The sharp clear light mixed well with the dancers and their costumes, and the shadows were sharp and clear as well, creating a perfect pattern for a successful painting. I established value relationships early in the painting with very dark washes, often leaving them as they are to prevent over-working any one area of the painting.

DOTTIE BURTON
Woman of Yugo
21.5" x 15.5" (55 cm x 39 cm)
Arches 140 lb.

Light was used to project the figure and was necessary for the compositional design of the painting, leading the viewer into, around, and out of the painting. My chosen colors were indicative of the feeling of the character and the somberness of the country and people of Yugoslavia before war broke out. The play of light on the figure and pigeons establishes interest within the work.

FRAN SCULLY
Afternoon Shadows
14.25" x 21.5" (36 cm x 55 cm)
Arches 140 lb. cold press
Watercolor with gouache

I was attracted to this scene by the horizontal band of shadows crossing the landscape. I visualized the painting using four bands of color crossing the paper, one for the sky, another for the distant hills, a band of dark shadows for the valley, and one for the lighter shadow of the roadside. Using transparent watercolor, I began wet-in-wet, gradually building up color and spattering to create texture. Additional color was included by dry glazing, with more texture added using drybrush and further spattering. Gouache was used for the thin lines of the foreground trees.

LINDA BACON
Eleven Eyes Have It
56" x 42" (142 cm x 107 cm)
Arches 140 lb. cold press

My main criteria for selecting or rejecting objects in a still life is the way light plays off and among them. Shiny reflective objects, translucent ones, objects that cast dramatic shadows, and objects that make striking reflections in other objects are my primary choices. I arrange and rearrange the objects with respect to the light source and each other. I experiment by shifting the light source and point of view, but usually use a single light source from the side for the most exciting shadows and highlights. Two-dimensional shapes take on the illusion of three-dimensional forms by combining light and shadow and exaggerating both.

RICHARD P. RESSEL
Lake Street
21" x 28" (53 cm x 71 cm)
Fabriano 300 lb. cold press
Watercolor with acrylic

I like painting the long shadows of winter combined with the shafts of light created by the breaks between buildings. Snow makes an everyday subject extraordinary— streets become a combination of frozen, wet, and dry surfaces which, when combined with shadows, bring interest to the painting. The challenge is to create dimension in the shadows, preventing them from becoming flat. I use acrylics in a transparent watercolor technique, slowly building cool washes to create depth. The permanence of acrylics allows me to build layers of washes, including wet-in-wet, without disturbing previous applications.

HENRY FUKUHARA
Could It Be Mexico?
24" x 18" (61 cm x 46 cm)
Winsor and Newton 140 lb.

Each time I've visited Mexico, I have been excited by the churches, walls, and people. There is a certain quality to the light that permeates the scene that is gloriously depicted with watercolor on paper. This is my interpretation of capturing that light, and in doing so, asking *Could It Be Mexico?* After doing value sketches, I painted directly on dry paper.

ALICE W. WEIDENBUSCH
French Mountains
10.75" x 14.5" (27 cm x 37 cm)
Winsor and Newton 140 lb.

The light, colors, shapes, and design of the distant landscapes remained fresh in my memory after a trip to the French countryside. Using photographs as reference, I created *French Mountains*. The design of the winding streets of the small town and the rooftops, long a fascination to me, suggest the foreground. The rhythm of color and shadows gives an abstract quality to the background.

ABOUT THE AUTHORS

PAINTING LIGHT AND SHADOW

Betty Lou Schlemm, *Judge*

Betty Lou Schlemm, A.W.S., D.F., has been painting for more than thirty years. Elected to the American Watercolor Society in 1964, and later elected to the Dolphin Fellowship, she has served as both regional vice president and director of the American Watercolor Society. Schlemm is also a teacher and an author. She has been conducting painting workshops in Rockport, Massachusetts, for twenty-nine years. Her book *Painting with Light,* published by Watson-Guptill in 1978, has remained a classic. She recently published *Watercolor Secrets for Painting Light,* distributed by North Light Books, Cincinnati.

Sara M. Doherty, *Editor*

Sara M. Doherty graduated from Knox College, in Galesburg, Illinois, and took graduate-level courses in education at Loyola University in Chicago. She has been a teacher and a learning center director, and she has helped organize a number of national art competitions, juried exhibitions, and painting workshops. She also worked on the production and sale of an art instruction video with noted watercolorist Sondra Freckelton. In 1994, Doherty accompanied a group of artists and art lovers to Italy and reported on the workshop in an article published in *American Artists* magazine.

DIRECTORY

Catherine Anderson **141**
4900 Trinity Road
Glen Ellen, CA 95442

Mary Ellen Andren **150**
8206 B Willowbrook Circle
Huntsville, AL 35802

Betty Lockhart Anglin **119**
213 Parkway Drive
Newport News, VA 23606

Coralie Armstrong **232**
P. O. Box 22
Inglewood, SA 5133
Australia

Linda Bacon **246**
Box 378
Ross, CA 94957

Hella Bailin, A.W.S. **155, 239**
829 Bishop Street
Union, NJ 07083

Carmen Newman Bammert **67, 123**
9116 Buffalo Court
Flushing, MI 48433

Aline Barker **105**
1137 Ash Street
Louisville, KY 40217

Margo Bartel **183**
3416 Bilglade Road
Fort Worth, TX 76133-1407

Miles G. Batt, Sr. **72**
301 Riverland Road
Ft. Lauderdale, FL 33312

Mary Ann Beckwith **144**
619 Lake Avenue
Hancock, MI 49930

Mary Jane Bell **149**
1018 D South 42nd Street
Birmingham, AL 35222

Pat Berger **173**
2648 Anchor Avenue
Los Angeles, CA 90064

June Berry **132**
45 Chancery Lane
Beckenham
Kent BR3 6NR
England

Dorothy W. Bertine, S.W.S.,
S.W.A., A.C.A. **210**
913 Chasewood Lane
Denton, TX 76205-8203

Judi Betts, A.W.S. **225**
P. O. Box 3676
Baton Rouge, LA 70821-3676

Jack B. Bevier, Estate of, **124**
811 West Alisal Street
Salinas, CA 93901

Donne F. Bitner **53, 112**
449 Blakey Boulevard
Cocoa Beach, FL 32931

Joseph Bohler, A.W.S. **142, 223**
P.O. Box 387
556 Trumbull Lane
Monument, CO 80132

Joan M. Boryta **165**
133 East Main Street
Plainfield, MA 01070

Marilyn Sears Bourbon **78**
16765 Oak View Circle
Morgan Hill, CA 95037

Jorge Bowenforbés, A.W.S,
N.W.S. **26, 179**
P.O. Box 1821
Oakland, CA 94612

Betty C. Boyle **121**
5081 South Poplar Drive
Columbus, IN 47201

Angela Bradburn **220, 221**
625 Shadow Brook Drive
Columbia, SC 29210

Robert W. Bragg **85**
4545 East Conway Drive NW
Atlanta, GA 30327

Charlotte Britton, A.W.S., N.W.S.
21
2300 Alva Avenue
El Cerrito, CA 94530

Jack R. Brouwer, A.W.S. **97, 184**
2231 Meadowglen Drive NE
Grand Rapids, MI 49505

Peggy Brown, A.W.S., N.W.S.
115
1541 North Claylick Road
Nashville, IN 47448

Daryl Bryant **171**
2309 La Engina Way
Pasadena, CA 91107

Magaret Ebbinghaus Burch **169**
Route 1 Box 287
Anderson, MO 64831

Madeleine Burke-Fanning **146**
4160 Rommitch Lane
Pensacola, FL 32504-4490

Dan Burt, A.W.S., N.W.S. **55**
2110 B West Lane
Kerrville, TX 78028-3838

Dottie Burton **244**
1916 Bay Hill Drive
Las Vegas, NV 89117

Ranulph Bye, N.A., A.W.S., D.F.
189
P. O. Box 362
Mechanicsville, PA 18934

Nel Byrd **206**
1933 Shadow Trail
Plano, TX 75075

Barbara George Cain **73**
11617 Blue Creek Drive
Aledo, TX 76008

S. Ohrvel Carlson **191**
43 Broadway
Rockport, MA 01966

Judy Cassab **117**
16/C Ocean Avenue
Double Bay
Sydney, 2028
Australia

Todd Chalk **45, 46**
4150 South Harris Hill Road
Williamsville, NY 14221

Chang Fee-Ming **136**
56–5/4 Pangsapuri Cerong Lanjut
20300 Kuala Terrengganu,
Terrengganu, Malaysia

Mary C. Chan, M.W.S. **116**
1555 Elm Street
Napa, CA 94559

Anna Chen **140**
691 Bear Creek Court
Winter Springs, FL 32708

Allison Christie **39, 188**
521 Spring Valley Road NW
Atlanta, GA 30318-2640

Celia Clark **27**
R.D. 2, Box 228 A
Delhi, NY 13753

Ruth Cocklin **114**
5923 South Willow Way
Englewood, CO 80111

Jean Cole **182**
78 Ash Street
Denver, CO 80220

Mari M. Conneen, N.W.S. **113**
441 North Harbor City Boulevard
Melbourne, FL 32935

Dede Coover **42**
3008 Twin Oak Road
Cameron Park, CA 95682

Naomi Cox **139**
330 South Lincoln Street
Burbank, CA 91506

Maxine Custer **160**
2083 Trevino Avenue
Oceanside, CA 92056

Mickey Daniels **27**
4010 East San Juan Avenue
Phoenix, AZ 85018

Jean Deemer, N.W.S. **156**
1537 Briarwood Circle
Cuyahoga Falls, OH 44221

Jack Denney **195**
700 A. Bordeaux Court
Elk Grove Village, IL 60007

Lorraine Denzler **23**
36728 32nd South
Auburn, WA 98001

Pat Dews, A.W.S., N.W.S. **234**
13032 S. E. Coghill Court
Hobe Sound, FL 33455

Brad Diddams **228**
1210 W. Tulane Drive
Tempe, AZ 85283

Henry W. Dixon, N.W.S., K.W.S.
48, 193
8000 East 118th Terrace
Kansas City, MO 64134

Brian Donn **11**
3364 Boundary Street
San Diego, CA 92104

Evalyn J. Dyer **74**
6041 Worrel Drive
Ft. Worth, TX 76133

Pauline Eaton **127**
68 Hop Tree Trail
Corrales, NM 87048

Deborah Ellis **243**
423 South Lee Street
Alexandria, VA 22314

Harriet Elson **198**
10 North Main Street
Munroe Falls, OH 44262

Nancy Feldkamp **10**
8701 Smyth Road
Manchester, MI 48158

Mary Lou Ferbert **84**
334 Parklawn Drive
Cleveland, OH 44116

Pat Fortunato **89**
70 Southwick Drive
Orchard Park, NY 14127-1650

Yolanda Frederikse **164**
9625 Dewmar Lane
Kensington, MD 20895

Jane Frey **38**
518 West Franklin
Taylorville, IL 62568

Henry Fukuhara **248**
1214 Marine Street
Santa Monica, CA 90405

Marsha Gegerson **44**
10241 Northwest 48 Court
Coral Springs, FL 33076

George Gibson, N.A., A.W.S.,
N.W.S. **118, 197**
1449 Santa Maria Avenue
Los Osos, CA 93402

James Gleeson **243**
148 Precita Avenue
San Francisco, CA 94110

Harriet Marshall Goode **37**
844 Myrtle Drive
Rock Hill, SC 29730

Barbara Goodspeed **233**
11 Holiday Point Road
Sherman, CT 06784-1624

Virginia L. Gould **130**
347 Hiawatha Terrace
Wood Dale, IL 60191

Irwin Greenberg **9**
17 West 67th Street
New York, NY 10023

Geraldine Greene **41**
102 Plantation Boulevard
Islamorada, FL 33036

Marilyn Gross **70**
374 MacEwen Drive
Osprey, FL 34229

Gerry Grout **94**
57 Biltmore Estates
Phoenix, AZ 85016

Linda S. Gunn **34**
5209 Hanbury Street
Long Beach, CA 90808

Ken Hansen, N.W.S. **242**
241 JB Drive
Polson, MT 59860

Robert E. Heyer **185**
102 Booream Avenue
Milltown, NJ 08850

Sharon Hildebrand **22, 93**
5959 St. Fillans Court W
Dublin, OH 43017

Allan Hill **147**
2535 Tulip Lane
Langhorne, PA 19053

Jane R. Hofstetter, N.W.S. **63**
308 Dawson Drive
Santa Clara, CA 95051

Carol Hubbard, A.W.S. **109**
574 Cutler's Farm Road
Monroe, CT 06468

Mary Sorrows Hughes **60**
1045 Erie Street
Shreveport, LA 71106

Amanda Jane Hyatt **229, 230**
25 Culzean Crescent
Highton 3216 Victoria
Australia

Diane Jackson **108**
P.O. Box 211
Montross, VA 22520

Vaughn L. Jackson **91**
11600 Ten Penny Drive
Fairfax Station, VA 22039

Emily James **148**
6917 Oakmont Parkway
Naples, FL 34108

Kathleen Jardine **66**
470 Tanager Lane
Chapel Hill, NC 27514

Edwin L. Johnson **227**
7925 N. Campbell Street
Kansas City, MO 64118-1521

Jane E. Jones **65**
5914 Bent Trail
Dallas, TX 75248

Zetta Jones **110**
105 North Union Street #6
Alexandria, VA 22314

Lola Juris **16, 17**
3200 Buena Hills Drive
Oceanside, CA 92056-3942

Jean Kalin, A.P.S.C., K.W.S. **168**
11630 NW 64th Street
Kansas City, MO 64152

Joyce H. Kamikura, F.C.A., N.W.S.
50
6651 Whiteoak Drive
Richmond, BC V7E 4Z7
Canada

M.C. Kanouse **125, 200**
308 Mill Street
P. O. Box 782
Sheridan, MT 50749

Nordia Kay **58**
145 Humphrey Street
Marblehead, MA 01945

Anne Kittel **98**
1263 Sunbury Drive
Fort Myers, FL 33901-8738

Judith Klausenstock **47**
94 Reed Ranch Road
Tiburon, CA 94920

George W. Kleopfer, Jr. **31**
2110 Briarwood Boulevard
Arlington, TX 76013

Pat Kochan **226**
3727 Blue Trace Lane
Dallas, TX 75244

George E. Kountoupis **176, 177**
5523 East 48th Place
Tulsa, OK 74135

James L. Koevenig **43**
845 Keystone Circle
Oviedo, FL 32765

Priscilla E. Krejci **180**
4020 Fiser
Plano, TX 75093

Fredrick Kubitz, A.W.S., N.E.W.S.
12, 170
12 Kenilworth Circle
Wellesley, MA 02181

Gertrude Lacy **20**
200 Fiddletop Lane
Covington, VA 24426

Janet Laird-Lagassee **15**
43 Elmwood Road
Auburn, ME 04210

Robert Lamell, K.A., N.W.O. **71**
2640 West Wilshire Boulevard
Oklahoma City, OK 73116

Monroe Leung, N.W.S., A.W.S.
101, 133, 186
1990 Abajo Drive
Monterey Park, CA 91754

Douglas Lew **35**
4382 Browndale Avenue
Edina, MN 55424

Nat Lewis **187**
51 Overlook Road
Caldwell, NJ 07006

Roberta P. Lintner **137**
7925 Ellet Road
Springfield, VA 22151

Fred MacNeill **126**
23 Dana Road
Concord, MA 01742

David Maddern **30**
6492 Southwest 22nd Street
Miami, FL 33155-1945

Ward P. Mann **166**
163 Stony Point Trail
Webster, NY 14580

Margaret R. Manring **172**
3713 Highland Avenue
Skaneateles, NY 13152

Daniel J. Marsula, A.W.S., M.W.S.
211
2828 Castleview Drive
Pittsburgh, PA 15227

Margaret M. Martin, A.W.S. **59**
69 Elmwood Avenue
Buffalo, NY 14201

Lena R. Massara **99**
3 Leeward Court
Salem, SC 29676

Karen Mathis **62**
9400 Turnberry Drive
Potomac, MD 20854

Benjamin Mau, N.W.S. **64**
1 Lateer Drive
Normal, IL 61761

Jule McClellan **205**
2805 Tippecanoe Trail
Henderson, KY 42420

Laurel Lake McGuire **134**
1914 Blueridge Road
Ridgecrest, CA 93555

Frances H. McIlvain **49**
40 Whitman Drive
Red Bank, NJ 07701

John McIver, A.W.S., N.W.S.,
W.H.S. **209**
P. O. Box 9338
Hickory, NC 28603

Joanna Mersereau **32, 181**
4290 University Avenue
Riverside, CA 92501

Frank J. Milauskas **161**
74 Wauchusett Avenue
Arlington, MA 02174

Robert T. Miller, A.W.I., F.V.A.S.
218
Unit 187 Cumberland View
Whalley Drive
Wheelers Hill, VIC 3150
Australia

Judy Morris, N.W.S. **216**
2404 East Main Street
Medford OR 97504

Sybil I. Moschetti **120**
1024 11th Street
Boulder, CO 80302

Sidney T. Moxham, S.E.A. **103**
7316 East McLellan Boulevard
Scottsdale, AZ 85250

Barbara Nechis **212**
1085 Dunaweal Lane
Calistoga, CA 94515

John A. Neff **154**
17 Parkview Road
Wallingford, CT 06492

Jean R. Nelson, W.H.S **111**
1381 Doe Street, NW
Christianburg, VA 24073

Lael Nelson **175**
600 Lake Shore Drive
Scoggins, TX 75480

Alice A. Nichols **238**
33002 Maplenut
Farmington, MI 48336

Beverly Perdue Nida **128**
2100 Albion Road
Midlothian, VA 23113

Paul W. Niemiec, Jr. **75, 208**
P.O. Box 674
Baldwinsville, NY 13027

Michael Nicholson **56**
255 South Brookside Drive
Wichita, KS 67218

Bea Jae O'Brien **135**
34 Sea Pines
Moraga, CA 94556

Jane Oliver **151, 236**
20 Park Avenue
Maplewood, NJ 07040

Robert S. Oliver, A.W.S., N.W.S.
40, 107, 192
4111 East San Miguel
Phoenix, AZ 85018

Don O'Neill, A.W.S. **237**
3723 Tibbetts Street
Riverside, CA 92506

Gloria Paterson, N.W.S. **54, 194**
9090 Barnstaple Lane
Jacksonville, FL 32257

Donald W. Patterson **138, 215**
441 Cardinal Court North
New Hope, PA 18938

Joyce F. Patrick **36**
P.O. Box 9347
Rancho Santa Fe, CA 92067

Kathleen Pawley, K.W.S. **159**
411 Creason Court #205
Louisville, KY 40223

Ann Pember **61, 196**
14 Water Edge Road
Keeseville, NY 12944

Jim Pittman **14, 90**
Box 430
Wakefield, VA 23888

Janet Poppe **240**
803 County Line Road
Highland Park, IL 60035

Alex Powers **86**
401 72nd Avenue, N., Apt. 1
Myrtle Beach, SC 29577

Dolores V. Preston **219**
165 Marian Parkway
Crystal Lake, IL 60014

L. Herb Rather Jr., A.W.S., N.W.S. **152**
M. Route 1 Box 89
Lampasas, TX 76550

Bev Reiley **131**
4311 State Route 138
Greenfield, OH 45123

Richard P. Ressel **247**
1010 Fountain Avenue
Lancaster, PA 17601

Patricia Reynolds, M.W.S. **13, 87**
390 Point Road
Willsboro, NY 12996

Michael P. Rocco, A.W.S. **224**
2026 S. Newkirk Street
Philadelphia, PA 19145

Raka Bose Saha **68**
1485 Country Lake Drive
Lilburn, GA 30247

Robert Sakson, A.W.S., D.F. **83, 167**
10 Stacey Avenue
Trenton, NJ 08618-3421

Betty Carmell Savenor **82**
4305 Highland Oaks Circle
Sarasota, FL 34235

Nicolas P. Scalise **241**
59 Susan Lane
Meriden, CT 06450

J. Juray Schaffner **79**
14727 Chermoore Drive
Chesterfield, MO 63017-7901

Ken Schulz, A.W.S. **201**
P. O. Box 396
Gatlinburg, TN 37738

Fran Scully **245**
170 East Street South
Suffield, CT 06078

Richard Seddon **76**
6 Arlesey Close
Lytoon Grove
London, SW15 2EX
England

Janet Shaffer **77**
11037 Timberlake Road
Lynchburg, VA 24502

George J. Shedd, A.W.S., A.A.A., N.E.W.S. **202, 203**
46 Paulson Drive
Burlington, MA 01803

Leona Sherwood **172**
615 Buttonwood Drive
Longboat Key, FL 34228

Morris J. Shubin **207**
313 North 12th Street
Montebello, CA 90640

Edwin C. Shuttleworth, F.W.S. **204**
3216 Chapel Hill Boulevard
Boynton Beach, FL 33435

Delda Skinner **33, 96**
8111 Doe Meadow Drive
Austin, TX 78749

Wayne H. Skyler **57**
20 Hickory Drive
Stanhope, NJ 07874

Dorla Dean Slider, A.W.S. **213, 214**
268 Estate Road
Boyertown, PA 19512

Patsy Smith, N.W.S. **153**
821 Apache Drive
North Platte, NE 69101

George Sottung, A.W.S. **231**
111 Tower Road
Brookfield, CT 06804

Linda L. Spies **145**
919 Coulter Street
Ft. Collins, CO 80524

Penny Stewart **8**
6860 Cedar Ridge Court
Colorado Springs, CO 80919

Betty M. Stroppel **100**
115 Sweetbriar Lane
North Plainfield, NJ 07060

Richard J. Sulea **106, 190**
660 East 8 Street
Salem, OH 44460

Fredi Taddeucci **95**
Route 1, Box 262
Houghton, MI 49931

Jane Talley **51**
8255 Carrick
Fort Worth, TX 76116

Virginia Abbate Thompson **174**
10776 S.W. 88 Street
Apt. F-21
Miami, FL 33176

Gregory B. Tisdale **199**
35 Briarwood Place
Grosse Point Farms, MI 48236

Nedra Tornay **69**
2131 Salt Air Drive
Santa Ana, CA 92705

Christine M. Unwin **29**
6850 Brookeshire Drive
West Bloomfield, MI 48322

Jan Upp **18, 19**
7335 Shadbleau
Jenison, MI 49428

Anthony Ventura **178**
3430 Highway 66
Neptune, NJ 07753

Wolodimira Vera Wasiczko **143**
5 Young's Drive
Flemington, NJ 08822

Donna L.Watson **157, 242**
19775 SW Taposa Place
Tualatin, OR 97062

Carolann Watterson **158**
4425 Van Noord Avenue
Studio City, CA 91604

Kitty Waybright **235**
1390 Bailey Road
Cuyahuga Falls, OH 44221

Alice W. Weidenbusch **249**
1480 Oakmont Place
Niceville, FL 32578-4314

Elaine Weiner-Reed **52**
1309 Bernie Ruth Lane
Severn, MD 21144

Judith Wengrovitz **102**
5220 Cather Road
Springfield, VA 22157

Elaine Wentworth **88**
132 Central Street
Norwell, MA 02061

Trudy M. Whitney **92**
4177 Hearthstone Drive
Sarasota, FL 34238-3205

Mary Wilbanks, N.W.S., W.V.S.A. **129**
18307 Champion Forest Drive
Spring, TX 77379

Joyce Williams, A.W.S., N.W.S. **217**
Box 192
Tenants Harbor, ME 04860

Douglas Wiltraut **222**
969 Catasauqua Road
Whitehall, PA 18052

Yvonne Wood **24, 25**
3 Babcock Road
Rockport, MA 01966

Ann Zielinski **104**
Ford Cove
Hornby Island BC V0R 1ZO
Canada

GLOSSARY

Analogous colors: the shades, tints, or tones of any three colors that are next to each other on the color wheel.

Background: the part of the painting that appears to be farthest from the viewer.

Balance: the even distribution of shapes and colors in a painting.

Bristol board: a stiff, durable cardboard made in plate and vellum finishes with thicknesses of one- to four-piles.

Cold-press paper: paper with a medium-rough texture as a result of being pressed with cold weights during processing.

Collage: process of constructing flat (or low relief) two-dimensional art by gluing various materials (i.e. newspaper, photographs, etc.) onto the painting surface.

Complementary colors: any two colors that are opposite each other on the color wheel (i.e., red and green), which create a high contrast when placed side by side.

Contrast: the juxtaposition of extremes within the compositions in colors (purple with orange), values (white with black), textures (coarse with smooth), etc.

Crayon resist: a technique in which crayon is applied to the surface and repels the paint that is applied afterward.

Crosshatching: brushstrokes applied at right angles to each other to create contrasting tone and density.

Dapple: to mark or patch with different shades of color.

Drybrush: a method of ink or watercolor painting in which most of the pigment has been removed from the brush before application.

Foreground: the part of the painting that appears to be closest to the viewer.

Gesso: a paste prepared from mixing whiting with size or glue and spread upon a surface to fit it for painting or gilding.

Gouache: a method of painting with opaque colors that have been ground in water and mingled with a preparation of gum.

Hot-press paper: paper with a smooth surface as a result of being pressed between calendar rollers that flatten the grain into an even finish.

Hue: the actual color of anything—also used to describe what direction a color leans toward, (i.e. bluish-green, etc.).

Illustration board: layers of paper adhered to a cardboard backing to produce a sturdy drawing surface, made in various thicknesses and textures.

Local color: the true color of an object seen in ordinary daylight.

Museum board: available in two- and four-ply, this soft, textured surface absorbs wet or dry pigment readily; usually used in archival matting and framing of artwork.

Saturation: the intensity or brightness of color.

Shade: the color achieved when black is added to a hue.

Spatter: to scatter color on the canvas by splashing on paint.

Stipple: to create an optical mix of colors through the use of dots or dashes.

Tint: the color achieved when white or water is added to a hue.

Tooth: refers to the depth of the grain of paper.

Value: the relative lightness or darkness of a color.

Vellum: a smooth, cream-colored paper resembling calfskin.

Wash: a thin, usually transparent coat of paint loosely applied to the surface of the canvas.